MW01165159

SUNRISE – SUNSET

Millie's *Divine* Journey

Autobiography by

Mildred E. Devine

Mildred E. Devine

COVER IMAGERY

FRONT COVER

My sister, Kathleen M. Devine, more affectionately referred to as *Katie,* upon her retirement, was getting back to her art work. The front cover is a print from one of her fabulous paintings. She was multi-talented in the arts ... music, painting, and literature.

I selected this particular painting for my cover because of its meaning to me. I see the seeds from the milkweed plant putting forth from its fat pods, laden with filaments as fine as silk, bursting and floating off into the air, and one never knowing where they will land; perhaps on a coat, a sleeve, or caught in one's hand, or replanting itself to create another of its own kind. I feel the same way about the people who have come into my lifetime. One never knows what impact you will have on someone else's life.

BACK COVER

A. Vincent Scarano is a highly imaginative, creative, and multi-talented photographer. His downtown New London, Connecticut studio is well-equipped and conveniently located approximately halfway between New York and Boston. His photography credits are worldwide: the New York Times, London Times, Bejing Daily News, Los Angeles Times, Washington Post, and others too numerous to list here.

He did the headshot photo that accompanies my brief bio. He also took the sunset photograph of the skyline of New London from the Thames River. He was aboard the Connecticut schooner Amistad, replica of an 1839 Cuban slave ship, the subject of a 1997 Steven Spielberg movie, *AMISTAD*. His works have been featured in exhibitions, television documentaries, advertising campaigns and brochures, educational textbooks, and architectural digests.

FOREWORD

For all of my life people have been having fun with my name by affording me such names as "the Divine Miss Millie" so I've decided to expand on that. I have a very strong faith; consequently, the sub-title of this book wherein I'm sharing my experiences through life and especially as I came up through the male-dominated banking field. I want to share with you the obstacles and opportunities experienced, realizing the importance of discernment and its amazing impact on my life.

It's important to me to share the history of what was happening in the 1970s and why we created the Southeastern Connecticut Women's Network and the Women's Center of Southeastern Connecticut, now known as Safe Futures, Inc. — both of which are now over 45 years old. Personally, I have nothing against men but have always believed that men and women are equal. We can all be very grateful for the fabulous visionaries and role models including Supreme Court Justice Ruth Bader Ginsberg and Gloria Steinham. We all owe them a debt of gratitude! Personally, I not only thank them but I salute them as well! When I recently saw the Documentary on Ruth Bader Ginsberg, I couldn't help think of Teddy Roosevelt and his famous quote: "Talk softly and carry a big stick; you will go far."

Most male clubs throughout our country and throughout the entire world have always been male exclusive. Women, if allowed to enter at all, could only slip in through another door, perhaps a back or lower portal, than the men. The men, of course, could boldly strut in through the main door -- or even if allowed to enter with the men, we women were not allowed to hang our coats with theirs, but we had to hang ours in the Ladies Room.

This was my firsthand experience of applying for the Eastern Connecticut Regional Trust Manager's position in 1987. This was the Bank for whom I was working. The Bank management felt the necessity not only to do a national search, which was normal, but also to interview the community to see if it was ready for a woman in that position. The overwhelming support I had from the mostly male business leaders was totally unbeknownst to me until after the Bank's decision was made.

My family had a very positive influence on my upbringing. My mom and her three sisters all shared a common life's motto: "Let me live in a house by the side of the road and be a friend to mankind." Our family's love of music and theater had a powerful impact on my life; consequently, the title of this book, taken from the fabulous musical FIDDLER ON THE ROOF and its refrain:

"Sunrise, Sunset, swiftly fly the years; one season following another, laden with happiness and tears."

Over my lifetime I've had the pleasure of working together with civic, social and cultural leaders helping to enhance our local communities. They provided key access to artistic events through the restoration and renovation of the fabulous Garde Arts Center. We were able to create the Community Foundation of Eastern Connecticut which benefits tax-exempt, non-profit entities. I became the founding mother of the Southeastern Connecticut Women's Network. Our Network members helped to create the Women's Center of Southeastern Connecticut now known as Safe Futures. I devote a whole chapter to the great things they have done to rescue so many women, children and men from domestic violence situations, control and manipulation issues, and the traumatic effects of bullying. The Women's Network and Safe Futures have partnered from the very beginning in 1976.

The magnitude of the individual and the collective impact made on thousands of people who have struggled over a lifetime and beyond is awesome and overwhelming to conceptualize. This story needs to be told to encourage our youth to attain their best. This book is intended to inspire and to assure them that they can dream big … and to bring those dreams to life.

As former First Lady Eleanor Roosevelt once said: "No one can make you feel inferior without your consent."

DEDICATION

I dedicate my autobiography to honor and to praise the steadfast, loving, caring workers, administrators, and board members of Safe Futures, Inc. It is important to recognize everything they do to keep people of both genders and all ages safe through preventive training and mandatory care of those dealing with domestic violence and bullying.

Proceeds from the sale of this book are ALL going to:

Safe Futures, Inc.,

16 Jay Street, New London, CT 06320

for the continuance and fulfillment of their vital mission:
providing services to women, children, and men
who are dealing with bullying, strangulation, and physical abuse.

CHAPTER 1

Welcome to My *Divine* Journey

Where to begin? I might as well start at the very beginning (as good a place as any to start). I was born to Edward and Mabel Devine in New London, Connecticut at Lawrence + Memorial Hospital, now a subsidiary of Yale-New Haven Healthcare. I am the younger of two daughters; my elder sister, by four years, was Kathleen, more lovingly known to family and friends as Katie.

For all who knew Katie, she was a tall and fun-loving lady. She was also a talented musician and an artist, having majored in piano and English in college. In fact, I used, for my book's front cover, a picture of a painting done by my beloved sister. The Milkweed Plant, with its fat pods of seeds, bursting and blowing those fine, silky filaments off into the wind – never knowing where they will land – reminds me of the *thousands of lives* we all touch throughout our time here. We never really know the impact we've made on other people's lives until occasionally someone in conversation mentions what you have done for them.

When we were very young, Katie couldn't wait for me to become old enough and tall enough so *I* could be the one dusting the rungs of the chairs and tables instead of her. We were a middle-income family. Our parents worked very hard. Mom was a school teacher and Pop worked for an IGA Store in the Cohanzie Section of Waterford, until after Katie and I were born. In the mid-1940s he became a salesman for Wonder Bread. He was delivering bread to the local grocery stores in the greater Norwich Area. In later years he changed to having a restaurant route in the greater Groton Area, which he was still doing in 1970 when he retired after twenty-five years. We were very proud of Pop and especially because he had a perfect driving record for a quarter of a century.

Mom and Pop met at the IGA Store in Cohanzie. Mom was teaching there in the elementary school at that time. She was putting on a play with the children and needed orange crates for props; so, she went to the local IGA store to see if they had any extras. It was there that she met Pop; they courted on and off for a number of years. They eloped and married on March 3, 1933 ("3/3/33" — an easy date to remember) in *St. Mary's, Star of the Sea Church Rectory* in New London. Of course, I always thought that was so romantic.

At the time of their elopement, Pop was working in Waterford, Connecticut and Mom was teaching in Asbury Park, New Jersey. They kept their marriage a secret until June, 1933, when school was out for the year. Otherwise, Mom would have lost her job. School systems at that time did *not* hire married women as teachers because they *might become pregnant.* Who could possibly imagine *a pregnant woman* in front of a classroom of young children!

In 1918 Mom's family moved to the Village of Quaker Hill in the northern end of Waterford. Mom was 11 years old. In the mid-1930s she and Pop acquired land from her sisters. That's where they built their home. It was completed within a year and they moved into it in September, 1937. Katie was born in January, 1938 during a snow storm; I came along four years later in yet another January snow storm. Believe it or not, I am still living in that beautiful homestead. I didn't expect to be in it all these years; but life often takes unexpected twists and turns regardless of what we may be anticipating.

When I was three years old, Mom went back to teaching first grade. Until I was old enough to go to school, age 6, I spent days with my Aunt Mildred and Uncle Laurence Minson on their dairy farm located on the Old Colchester Road in Montville.

As a child, I often got carried away creating imaginary pets and playmates. My parents, of course, knew nothing of this passion. You see, our home was surrounded by woods. We didn't have any close neighbors with children. Yes, I did play with dolls and paper cut-outs like any girl; but I often found myself playing school where I was the classroom teacher of imaginary students. I even had papers to correct in math and spelling.

4

I also loved riding my bicycle all over our yard. Pop and I would either play basketball with a hoop-and-net he installed on the front of the garage, or sometimes we'd play softball. As a family, we enjoyed croquet, board games, and cards. Our parents scrimped and saved enough so we could join the "elite" *by purchasing our first television set ...* a rare privilege in the early 1950s. Back then, youth also enjoyed special children's characters such as 'Howdy Doody,' 'Buffalo Bob,' and 'Clarabelle the Clown;' later these were followed by the Mickey Mouse Club with its popular Mouseketeers.

From the time I started receiving an allowance of twenty-five cents per week, I had my own little black book where I kept track of what I received and how it was spent.

Mom was actually my first-grade teacher. We were a class of thirty-eight students, one teacher, no aides or assistants. It was also the same year part-time Kindergarten was started in Quaker Hill. I used to tease Mom that while I was progressing, she was regressing. I moved on to second grade to another teacher; but that second-grade teacher would only take thirty of the thirty-eight students. So ... Mom was assigned a split-class of first-grade students, plus eight second-graders as well. By the time I moved on to third grade, the kindergarten teacher job had become full-time with thirty children in the morning and thirty in the afternoon. That's when Mom made the switch to teaching Kindergarten. She remained in that position for the next twenty years until retiring in 1970.

I am proud to say I am a product of the Waterford Public School System from first through twelfth grade. I was one of 155 graduating seniors from the first class of Waterford High School in 1960. Having your mother teaching in the same system can be challenging — not from her standpoint, but from the standpoint of many teachers over the years. For some reason, other faculty members always expected more because "your mother is a teacher." Consequently, often you were *not* given the same treatment or privileges as the other children. In other words, it did not meet *The Four Way Test*. In my opinion, as well as that of *The*

Test, it was not fair to all concerned, especially to us students with parents teaching in the same system.

You may not be aware of The Four Way Test. Neither was I until I joined New London Rotary. It is a motto the Rotarians all live by. This reminder to Rotarians is recited at their meetings as one we all should live by:

> Of the things we think, say or do:
> 1. Is it the TRUTH?
> 2. Is it FAIR to all concerned?
> 3. Will it build GOOD WILL AND BETTER FRIENDSHIPS?
> 4. Will it be BENEFICIAL to all concerned?"

***

Now, let's return to telling you about our continued Waterford schooling. It was exciting being the lead class during our journey through the new high school, because we established so many traditions for what would one day become our *alma mater.* We got to name the athletic teams the *Lancers.* One of our classmates actually wrote our school song, while another one designed the logo. We, of course, chose our school colors, too.

My older sister graduated from New London High School in 1955, which was their first graduating class. NLHS combined the former private boys' schools of Chapman Tech and Bulkeley High, along with girls from Williams Memorial Institute. New London High served not only New London students, but those from Waterford, East Lyme, and Montville as well. It wasn't long after that merger, the Williams Memorial Institute, which had been the girls' high school for this area, changed its name to The Williams School. It was later moved to the Connecticut College campus.

Katie had similar experiences to mine with mom teaching in the same system. She was looking forward to going to New London High. Unfortunately for Katie, things did not change. When she arrived in New London, only the players were different. Instead of mom teaching in the New London School System, our wonderful and highly regarded aunts taught there.

Let me digress and share with you a little about our dear aunts. Mom was the youngest of the four Sistare sisters. I've already told you about Aunt Mildred, for whom I was named. Our aunts Grace and Gertrude had each taught in overcrowded, tiny one-room schools in Waterford. To boot, this encompassed grades one through eight. In later years, Aunt Grace became Principal of the old Winthrop Elementary School in New London, where she proved to be a trailblazer in *special education.*

Aunt Gertrude -- known more affectionately to us as 'Aunt Trudy' -- became Principal of Quaker Hill Elementary School. She later finished her career as an educator teaching English and math at Jennings Junior High School in New London.

Needless to say, we come from a long line of teachers in our family.

I have always had a passion for math, English, and music, but wasn't the best in history or science. I found history fascinating, but had a hard time retaining it. I did take the college-prep courses in high school, but when given electives, I opted for typing, shorthand, and accounting. My thinking was, even if I got married, I'd always have secretarial skills on which to fall back. While I graduated academically 10th in my class of 155, I wasn't eligible for the National Honor Society due to the *business subject electives*. Personally, neither my advisor nor I thought that was fair. You see, back in the 1950s there were basically three tiers of programs available: college prep -- consisting of academics and liberal arts -- business, or general studies. There were a lot of teachers and administrators at the time who were *old school* and harbored a built-in bias that students should *not* cross the lines between those program tiers. I was allowed to be on the honor roll, while in other schools only the *college-prep* students were so recognized. Even though I was a college prep student, I was not eligible for the National Honor Society ... recognition being reserved for only the "top tier" of students.

I was truly honored and elated at graduation that my classmates had voted me *the most likely to succeed in business*. I was particularly pleased with that special acknowledgement, because business subjects delve into society's ever-changing economies in great depth. My childhood memories take me back to keeping the Little Black Book in which I tracked my allowance and how it was either saved or spent. When I took the accounting course, I learned in the financial world that what I had been doing was actually more appropriately called *debits and credits.* This bookkeeping process is the means used in tracking one's *income and expenses,* whether personal or business. I have always been a highly detail-oriented and pragmatic individual. Consequently, I thought it mandatory to prepare myself for transitioning into the real world.

During my high school years, I worked part-time in the Credit Department of the now defunct Sears, Roebuck & Company in the New London Shopping Center. In fact, I recall one evening, Mr. Howser, the credit manager, coming out of his office and asking everyone, "Who knows algebra?" By then I had had two years of algebra studies and absolutely loved it! Thus, I enthusiastically offered to be of help to him. I did not realize at the time that he was trying to teach a young lady the practical use of what I was already learning in high school. *It worked.* I always treasured Mr. Howser's natural way of demonstrating the practical application of what most of us considered "academics."

Interestingly enough, much later in life our paths crossed again when I had an opportunity to let him know how much it had meant to me. I saw from his reaction that he was touched by my remembrances and that I had shared them with him.

CHAPTER 2

Life Transitions: early to mid-1960s

Upon graduation from Waterford High, I went off to Central
Connecticut State College, in New Britain, Connecticut, which
today is Central Connecticut State University. I was inspired by
my wonderful mentor, Arthur Hadfield, Ph.D., so my goal was to
follow in his footsteps and become a business education teacher. It
was not a good experience going from a small high school to a
much larger student population. I tried seeking guidance from my
faculty advisor with whom I had made an appointment; but she
didn't keep it. It seems she was meeting, instead, with her *pet
students,* who were known to be her favorites. By the time she
finished her session with them, she acknowledged me by saying
she just couldn't meet then because her mother was waiting for her
in the parking area. She had a way of making one feel unworthy of
her valuable time. I can assure you that was not only upsetting to

me, but frustrating, as well. However, I decided to make an appointment with the Dean for guidance. Unfortunately, that was not helpful either. All she did was put a box of tissues in front of me and told me, "Have a good cry for yourself and you'll feel better."

I am reminded of Eleanor Roosevelt's famous quote: "No one can make you feel inferior without your consent." I refused to be belittled and so moved on. Thus, I went to a pay phone, called my parents, and told them what had happened. I was then in the beginning of the second semester of my first year. I let my parents know that I just was not getting anywhere at Central Connecticut State College and I needed to come home. I also told them I felt badly that they would most likely lose money through this investment. I explained that I could always go back to work in the credit department of Sears, which is precisely what I did.

Of course, throughout that spring of 1961, Mom kept after me, letting me know that I wasn't going to work at Sears for the rest of my life. I needed to go on to further my education. By then,

Little Miss Independent had had a taste of the real world -- independence with her own income. But ... I also listened to Mom and found a work-study program in Boston. Pop had Wednesdays off from work. He drove me to Boston to interview at the Cambridge School of Business, and to explore possibilities for housing. I was accepted into the one-year Executive Secretarial Work-Study Program. We found a room in a private home in Brookline where I could stay.

***

Work-Study was actually a two-year program, but because of all the business courses I had taken as electives in high school, I was able to complete it in a single year. The program started in September, 1961. Through the school, I secured work with Hubbs Engine Company on Commonwealth Avenue in the Allston Section of Boston. I went to school mornings, and worked part-time afternoons. Upon graduation, I stayed on full-time as a secretary for the Parts & Service Departments.

We didn't have computers at that time; consequently, all of the dunning letters had to be individually typed by yours truly on a *manual* typewriter. As I recall, there were three levels of those letters, depending upon how late the customer was in remitting payments. Needless to say, typing the same letter over and over again got to be extremely boring and tedious. It was easy to let your mind wander.

One day, I was typing like mad, trying to get all those letters done, when suddenly I realized I had made a mistake! When I went to correct the typo, I discovered that I hadn't put any stationery in the typewriter. Unbeknownst to me, the boss was standing behind me and saw what was happening, including the missing letterhead. When I stopped to make the correction, he asked, "What made you stop?" I told him I had made an error and that I had corrected it. We both laughed and he added, "I thought maybe you were going to put a stamp on the platen and mail it."

It was a wonderful experience working in Boston for that company. I do not recall how many men worked there but there were a lot. I do know there were only six women working in this predominantly male engineering firm: the office manager, the bookkeeper, the secretary to the sales department, the switchboard operator, the parts & service secretary, and one general secretary.

We were paid on a weekly basis and each week we women would set aside a small amount of cash into a private expense fund. When we had accumulated enough money to cover the cost of taxis, we'd take ourselves out for dinner and a live show at a night club, where we saw some big-name performers. Great fun!

Living, going to school, and working in Boston were wonderful experiences. While attending school and living in a private home, along with the owners, two other students and I would walk to the MTA stop on Beacon Street. Today the MTA is now actually the Massachusetts Bay Transportation Authority, or MBTA – referred to as the "T." We would see a lot of the same people at that time taking the "T" into Boston for either work or school. I met a lot of people that way.

***

Since we were all living in different rooming houses, with no kitchen privileges, we would often see each other again in the evening, while eating at the Busy Bee Restaurant. My school mate's two brothers, both handsome with dark hair, also lived in that vicinity, but in different rooming houses. She introduced me to them and to a young, friendly blonde lady with a magnetic smile, at the "T" stop. It didn't take long to realize that a romance was brewing between this young lady and my school mate's eldest brother. This wonderful couple, Beryl and Charlie, did eventually marry. We became dear friends; their children becoming the closest I ever came to having a niece and a nephew.

Upon graduation from the Cambridge School of Business, my classmate and I took an apartment together for a year. During that time, I made my first cherry pie which included all of the lattice work. I just had to take a picture of it. After the picture was taken, the two of us ate the pie. It was delicious. Of course, we tried other recipes as well. My roommate was from Maine and brought with her two-family recipes -- one for salmon loaf and the other for fish chowder – both delicious.

By the end of that year, I moved to an efficiency apartment on Commonwealth Avenue, down the hall from my dear friends, Beryl and Charlie. Charlie had a passion for photography; on many an evening he'd work in his dark room. Beryl and I would get on the phone and gab for at least an hour about what was happening in Boston, world events, romances in which I was involved, work experiences, and usually the weather. Beryl and I could discuss anything, sharing our inner most feelings and secrets.

When Charlie wasn't working on photography in his dark room, occasionally we would all go out for an evening. We loved going to the Boston Pops concerts held on the banks of the Charles River, especially the July 4th performance with its fabulous fireworks and the *1812 Overture*, complete with roaring cannons. This was about 1963-64 when people actually dressed up to go out for an evening. One particular night we decided to get all *gussied up,* or in today's terms, *dressed up.* We went out to dinner, then to a movie. If memory serves me right, it was *It's a Mad, Mad, Mad World* with a motley assortment of characters embarking on a chaotic and slapstick filled race to find $350,000 in buried loot. We were definitely looking for something entertaining. It was. The film got out around 11:00 P.M. If you had to use public transportation at that time, you needed to be at your destination before midnight.

We'd hurried to catch the reliable old T, one of the last trolleys on that night's schedule. As it turned out, I was the last one to board that trolley … standing room only, as usual. I breathed a sigh of relief, as the conductor immediately closed the door behind me.

The T was not known for smooth starts, only disruptive ones. The ride was often a challenge especially if you were standing, as one risked falling into other passengers, or rubbing shoulders with some of the more unsavory characters, who always took the more underground passageways. God forbid, one should miss that last trolley and be forced to hoof it home through the midnight shadows or wait an eternity to catch an available taxi, never mind the added expense.

Thinking back to the trolley in those days and of the old Metropolitan Transit Authority, I'm reminded of a fun-loving song by the Kingston Trio: *M.T.A.* It was created as the Boston City Council was debating adding a tax and raising the T fares at that time. We really were entertained by that song, because the man referred to in it was called *Charlie.* The lyrics:

"Well, did he ever return?
No, he never returned and his fate is still unlearned
(What a pity)
He may ride forever 'neath the streets of Boston
He's the man who never returned ..."

(I prayed that fate would not befall me too.)

Most fondly, I recall the lovely, gracious, and beautiful Loretta Young, a movie star who started her career as a child actress in the 1920s. Later she transitioned from pretty child actor to one of Hollywood's foremost leading ladies in the 1930s and '40s. She won an Oscar for her role in *The Farmer's Daughter,* and was one of the first female stars to command a six-figure salary.

After retiring from her movie career, Miss Young became one of the first major Hollywood stars to build a successful career in the fledgling medium of *television*. In 1953 she signed a contract with NBC to produce and star in her own weekly, dramatic anthology television show. *The Loretta Young Show* ran for eight seasons from 1953 to 1961 with riveting suspense.

She played a major role in each of its diverse dramas, such as *Little Witness,* wherein Miss Young portrayed a mother struggling to protect her son, who had witnessed a murder. Another of her shows was the *Lady Killer* in which she starred as a mystery writer who becomes involved in a drama of mistaken identity. A third episode was *Count of Ten* in which she plays the critically ill wife of a retired boxer who re-enters the ring to raise money for a life-saving operation. All great shows.

Needless to say, I was an impressionable, yet mature young lady about to enter my teens and really noticing styles and fashions. Loretta Young was glamorous and would enter each show in a flourish of fashion by twirling through the doorway with her full skirt flaring. She graciously greeted the viewers and provided a brief introduction, setting the stage for that night's wonderfully intriguing episode. I was taken in with her flourishes and fashions. I was a huge fan of hers and tried emulating her grace and style. It did not go quite as planned.

I had my *'Loretta Young moments',* one of which was on that late night T ride coming from the movies in Boston. I recall that evening wearing my own *Loretta Young* coat. It was white with a stand-up collar, full skirt, and three-quarter-length sleeves. Of course, I just had to wear long black gloves with it, just like Loretta, as well as black-patent-leather-*spike* heels. You can just imagine that particular Loretta Young moment as the conductor began moving the trolley car, which started with a jolt. I grabbed the pole with my gloved hand, and swung around in true Loretta

Young fashion, only to find myself winding up sitting in some unsuspecting young-man's lap! I turned at least twenty shades of red, mortifying the bewildered young man who got off at the next stop. I'll never know if that was really his stop, or if he was so utterly embarrassed that he chose to exit at the next possible one. A gentleman got up and gave me his seat. My dear friends, Charlie and Beryl, who were with me at the time, pretended they didn't know me. From that point on, Charlie would always say, "You can come with us, *if* you behave yourself."

***

It was an adventure and quite the experience living in Boston, which to me was a big small town. We were always running into people we knew. Just look at the number of wonderful universities and colleges there. In addition to the well-known mammoth ones of Harvard and Boston University, there are Berklee College of Music, Emerson, Northeastern, and Tufts ... just to name a few.

I use to love walking to the Isabella Stewart Gardiner Museum on Sunday afternoons to see the latest art exhibit. My senses were awakened with their historic art collections, magnificent court yard, and exquisite instrumental musical performances. This unmistakable treasure is a hidden gem in Boston, about a block from the Museum of Fine Arts, and a short distance from Fenway Park, home of our beloved Red Sox. I would enjoy their latest art show that featured the likes of Rembrandt and Vermeer along with sketches by Degas, accompanied by a variety of classical musical ensembles ... my love was for the stringed instruments: violins and violas.

I was devastated in March, 1990 when I read about the thirteen masterpieces stolen, including the Rembrandts, Vermeer and sketches by Degas, from this fabulous unique museum. This theft was not only our country's largest property crime, but the world's most lucrative art heist. The total value of those stolen pieces was over $500 million. How sad ... to this day not one of those masterpieces has been retrieved.

As a youngster, I studied piano and violin, and was first violinist in the Clark Lane Junior High School Orchestra. I also sang in their chorus. Unfortunately, the brand-new high school didn't have an orchestra. Of course, one doesn't play a violin in the school marching band. Thus, I lost interest in playing the violin and gained more in going to dances, parties, and other fun events … like dating.

While attending Waterford High School, I also performed in the chorus. I always sang first soprano. I loved singing and still do to this day. In addition, I had the honor of singing in the school's unique Madrigal Singers, our octet, performing a cappella. A madrigal is a secular vocal music composition of the mid-1600s era. The number of voices can range from two to eight, most frequently three to six. Madrigals originated in Italy during the 1520s and became their most important secular music. The *madrigal* reached its formal and historical zenith by the second half of the 16th century. After the 1630s, the madrigal began to merge into other forms of music. In the 17th century, the opera with its infamous arias gradually displaced the madrigal.

While in high school I utilized my acting abilities by modeling my performances after Loretta Young's. I joined the Waterford High Dramatics Club and became a member of the National Thespian Society. It was great fun playing different parts. I generally was designated to the roles of a more mature woman. I came by that naturally since I was the youngest in my family.

***

Living in a big city is not always fun. There can be some scary times one never forgets; such as, the two-full year reign of terror caused by *The Boston Strangler*. It took place right when we were living in Boston. The span began in June 1962 and ended in January 1964. Unfortunately, there were thirteen single women victims, all living in different apartments throughout Boston. Each was found with her own nylon stockings wrapped several times around her neck and tied with a bow. The ages of the victims ranged from 19 to 85. All were sexually assaulted.

Buildings were all secured by such strict standards for those days and none of the apartments showed any signs of breaking and entering. Consequently, the investigators deduced that the victims knew their attacker; or that his ruse was sufficiently clever enough to allow him to gain entry into their apartments. (Sleep was surely disrupted by tossing and turning throughout the night during those uncomfortable times.)

One dreary evening, my dear friend Beryl had a frightening experience on the way back to her apartment house. She was walking alone on a tree-lined side street that was not brightly lit due to long spaces between the street lights. She was walking away from the trolley and feared she was being followed. As she heard footsteps and heavy breathing behind her, it seemed those feet were gaining on her … barely a step behind. She heard a tapping noise every other footstep. Beryl didn't know what that tapping was. Perhaps the interloper was carrying a large umbrella with a metal tip on its end and using it as a cane. Or, maybe he had a gun in his pocket and was tapping it with his ring. She kept picking up the pace until practically in an all-out run.

You can imagine the thoughts racing through her mind. Was it the Boston Strangler? Was she going to be raped … or killed?

Eventually whoever it was must have realized his presence had frightened her. "I won't harm you!" he shouted, nearly right on her heels. The sound of his voice so close to her terrified her all the more. Beryl saw her apartment building looming just ahead of her and dashed up the steps. Trembling she flung open the door, swung it shut and locked it. Safe at last.

Beryl's chilling episode gave us all the more cause for alarm when the media reported that the Strangler often gained entry by sliding a friendly note under the door. Initially, one would think the note was from a friend or neighbor. Needless to say, if someone rapped on your door, you didn't comply automatically by opening it. One evening such a note came under *my first-floor* efficiency apartment door. Being alone, I was alarmed. The note didn't make much sense, but seemed harmless enough. I still refused to open the door. (Would you have done so?)

In October 1964, a young woman reported that a man claiming to be a detective tied her to her bed and began raping her. But then he stopped suddenly, apologized, and left. Her description led police to believe that Albert DeSalvo was the assailant. And when DeSalvo's actual picture was released in the newspapers, several women came forth accusing him of sexually assaulting them. However, the only attempted strangulation survivor, in reviewing a line-up with the detective, identified *another man* as her attacker … one George Nassar. Did the Greater Boston Area have more than one alleged murderer on its hands? It is said that DeSalvo confessed to the murders to fellow inmate George Nasser, who, in turn, notified his famous lawyer, F. Lee Bailey. The strangulations stopped, following DeSalvo's confession, but he was not officially charged because there was insufficient corroboration.

To this day, if you were to ask Bostonians who was *The Boston Strangler or Silk-Stocking Murderer,* you probably would hear the name Albert DeSalvo. One story had it that Nasser was the actual murderer, but convinced DeSalvo to confess to the crimes so Nasser would get the reward. It is also alleged that Nasser made a deal with DeSalvo that if he confessed, DeSalvo's wife would receive part of the reward money.

At the request of Nasser, Attorney F. Lee Bailey did take the DeSalvo case but ended up representing him on the *Green Man crimes,* which covered the 300 assaults on women where he always dressed in green. He was found guilty and received a life sentence.

We were all very relieved when the outcomes of each case were resolved, both men in prison for life. The strangulations ceased. Of course, we never did find out the truth of who was the actual *Boston Strangler:* Nasser or DeSalvo? It is said that DeSalvo was interviewed for a book on *The Boston Strangler,* in which he might have told us, but DeSalvo's life was cut short in 1973 when another Walpole Prison inmate stabbed him to death.

31

Had he lived, would he have told us who did it?

CHAPTER 3

Furthering My Career

Thankfully, having survived the terrors of the Boston Strangler, our lives returned to normal. I continued working at Hubbs Engine Company for a total of three-and-a half years; both as a student during the school year 1961-62 and then as full-time secretary 1962-65. The company moved to Woburn, Massachusetts on Route 128 in the fall of '64. For me it meant I needed to move on, closer to the new location. I found an efficiency apartment in Waltham. That town did not provide any public trains or other transportation to get us to Woburn. Consequently, it meant I had to buy a car, pay the same compulsory insurance as boys for being under age twenty-five, and commute to Woburn. All those added expenses *with no increase in pay*. Mom and Pop made it easy for me. They gave me her car, a Ford Futura, white exterior and red interior. It was a great little car.

When I was home during Christmas, I spoke with Pop about the work situation. I was torn because I liked working at Hubbs Engine. I didn't feel that I should call in sick to go looking for another job, but it was *costing me money to work there.* I had had to dip into principal, which I definitely knew was a *no-no.* Pop and I were very close. He suggested that I go back and give them a month's notice, because they had been so good to me. My Dad advised me to move back home. He also suggested I take two weeks for vacation, since I wouldn't be granted any in my first year of employment. Of course, once I was working, I would also begin paying rent. It all made perfect sense to me, although I had never even thought about moving home. I had never even considered it as an option. I was under the impression that once you were on your own, that was it -- *no turning back.*

I followed his sage advice, went back, gave a month's notice, and moved home during the foggy and snowy January, 1965. When I arrived, Pop said he thought a bank would be a nice place for a young lady to work. He had spoken with his local bank branch manager and was given the name of the personnel manager, which he offered me as a possibility. I appreciated his thoughtfulness; but again, *Little Miss Independent* here had to do it *her way*.

Instead, I started responding to employment ads in the New London Day newspaper, going for interviews, and just wasn't finding anything that really suited me. So, I went to the State Unemployment Office in New London. When I told the clerk I was out of work, immediately she started discussing unemployment benefits. I interrupted her, saying, "No. I left my prior job; I am looking for work!"

"Oh!" the clerk said, somewhat surprised, and redirected me to a person who handled opportunities for employment.

The interviewer for job referrals said the agency had a bank looking for a secretary. I asked "Which bank?" She said she couldn't tell me unless I agreed to go for the interview. I said, "I'll go for the interview." Lo and behold, it was with Catherine

MacLeod, Personnel Manager with Hartford National Bank and Trust Company in New London. Oh, yes, *the very same person* to whom Pop had referred me. Of course, the agency told me that the bank was looking for someone at least twenty-five years old. Since I was only twenty-three, they weren't sure I would be hired. Just the same, they sent me for the interview.

While I had plenty of confidence in my maturity and my skills going into the unemployment agency, their last comment left me worried and pondering some questions as I walked the long two blocks up the street and into the bank for the interview:

Would I really lose out on this potential job because I wasn't two years older? Wouldn't my schooling and secretarial skills be enough to impress them into hiring me? Up until then, I'd always been placed in more mature roles in high school plays, because everyone took me for being much older.

I walked those two blocks and went into the bank to meet with Miss MacLeod, an older, gray-haired lady. She'd obviously been with the bank for a long time. I found her formal, but welcoming. The position advertised was for a secretary in the trust department. I handed her my resume. As Miss MacLeod sat back in her chair, while perusing my credentials, she was so incredibly stoic. I could not read her impressions. It was nerve wracking.

When she finished reading it, she leaned back in her chair and said, "My, you have very impressive credentials. I see you are a member of the National Secretaries Association and have become a certified professional secretary." She elaborated, fully aware of the requirements needed to achieve that significant designation -- which had entailed sitting for a two-day, twelve-hour proctored examination. She further added, "I am not concerned that you know nothing yet about what a trust department actually does. *You will learn*."

I hoped and prayed that I would learn. I certainly did not want to disappoint Miss McLeod and her expressed confidence in me.

I also owned up to what the agency had told me regarding age. Miss Macleod said she may have requested from the agency "someone mature," but without specifying an actual age. We both agreed her request most likely had been interpreted as *age twenty-five plus*.

She added: "Young lady, your obvious sense of maturity and credentials have impressed me. Let me show you the trust department, where you will be working."

She walked me to the back of the bank's first floor to see the trust department. I was impressed by the beautiful office with gorgeous artwork above the wood paneling and those mammoth wooden desks. We didn't step into the office nor meet any of the officers and employees, which surprised me. She indicated I would be a secretary in that office. I accepted the position on the spot!

I began working for the bank the following Monday, March 8, 1965. Obviously, I was grateful there was no age discrimination policy at that time.

In my excitement, you can just imagine, I high-tailed it home to tell my parents that I had a job and where I would be working. In my exuberance, I told them the story of what had happened. Wearing a big grin, I told them about my successful interview with the stoic Miss MacLeod. I'm sure they had had a good hardy laugh about being right once again, but they never said "we told you so" regarding Dad's referral to Miss MacLeod.

***

Of course, much of this I attribute to my personal beliefs. I have always been a person of faith. I respect others' beliefs and religious preferences and never sit in judgment regarding anyone else's religion ... or lack of. Over the years I've come to believe there are no coincidences in life. I believe God has a plan for each of us.

I learned the trust and estate business from the ground up, with all of its intricate details. In this field, you are helping others. What could be better? It is where my passion for the business took roots. It also helps if you are a detail-oriented individual. That can be either a blessing or a curse, depending upon your viewpoint at the time.

Let me share with you what a trust department actually does. A wide variety of trusts exist. Trusts are legal documents created either by individuals, corporations, or the court system. In a trust department I have always dealt with personal and court-directed trusts versus corporate ones. The individual creating the trust determines if the agreement will be revocable or irrevocable – meaning, a revocable agreement can be amended; an irrevocable one cannot. In these documents one designates a trustee. This trustee may be either an individual, such as a member of the family -- or a friend, an attorney, an accountant, a bank that has trust powers, or an actual trust company.

For example, in my own estate planning, I have established an amendable and revocable trust. I am my own trustee for as long as I'm capable. When the time comes that I can no longer handle my own affairs, due to illness or death, I have appointed a successor trustee. I have registered all of my assets in the name of my trust, over which I have absolute control. Upon my passing that personal trust will become irrevocable. That means the trust cannot be changed in any way; thus, protecting the estate. I have the assurance that my instructions will be followed. The successor trustee will then distribute the assets according to my directions in that agreement.

There may be similarities in the format of trust & will documents, but the intricate details of each situation make the estate plan unique and adaptable to the individual who creates it. It is important to work with an attorney specializing in estates & trusts in order to capture the nuances of the individual's and family's idiosyncrasies, as well as personal charitable inclinations.

This personal business is one situation where you should *not* go online and try doing it yourself with such documents. We have seen too many circumstances in do-it-yourself situations where the estate spends more money to straighten out the mess after the death of a family member. If the decedent had gone to an estate planning attorney in the first place, the documents would have been properly drawn and a substantial sum of money would have been saved.

Trusts are created for a wide variety of varying purposes:

Irrevocable Trusts *cannot* be amended nor revoked. For example, individuals have created such trusts in memory of a family member -- but for charitable purposes. Examples include private foundations created by individuals that may benefit family members, such as, the Bodenwein Public Benevolent Foundation and the Frank Loomis Palmer Fund. Their trusts are the defenders of family members and the community they so loved, from people who do *not* have their best interest at heart. These trusts protect them from the power, status, and wizardry of such people as immortalized by the movie *Wall Street* and its legendary, notorious Gordon Gekko, played brilliantly by Michael Douglas.

***

I learned about private foundations, from the ground up, when I started working for Hartford National Bank & Trust

Company in March of 1965. As a secretary in the trust department, one of my first jobs was to post to 3" x 5" index cards the grants made to each non-profit charitable organization awarded by the Bodenwein Public Benevolent Foundation and the Frank Loomis Palmer Fund. A big part of my life has been involved working with non-profits, community, and private foundations. Allow me to share with you some definitions and historical background on these two special funds, which have contributed millions of dollars to our diverse community.

As you are no doubt aware, businesses deemed *for-profit* often have stockholders who invest in the corporation and who also receive dividend benefits from their investments. On the other hand, non-profit entities can operate as for-profits by reinvesting their net proceeds, based on the nature of their individual missions. Service organizations like Rotary Clubs and Chambers of Commerce all operate in this manner. Other non-profits operate solely for charitable purposes, such as religious, scientific, or educational. These two particular private foundations were created

43

by loving, caring individuals. They serve as a means of giving back to the communities that had meant so much to them and to their families.

Let me tell you a little about the individuals immortalized by such foundations:

Theodore Bodenwein was born in Dusseldorf, Germany in 1864. Due to the unpleasant and difficult living conditions at that time in Dusseldorf, many people migrated to America. His father immigrated to Connecticut in 1868, settling first in Groton, then in New London, where he worked as a shoemaker. At age 5, Theodore and his mother followed his father to the United States. At the time, the city of New London was struggling to find a new identity, given the decline of the whaling industry in the 1860s. (So prominent in Southeastern Connecticut is the moniker for the city of New London -- *The Whaling City* and New London High School's is *The Whalers.)*

For history buffs, it should be noted that during the period 1861-70 approximately 800,000 Germans immigrated to the United States. It was understood by immigrants that our streets were *paved with gold.* This old cliché meaning -- America was the land of opportunity. When I think of immigrants coming to America and landing on our shores, I immediately think of the Statue of Liberty and its famous quote taken from the poem *New Colossus* by Emma Lazarus:

"Give me your tired, your poor,
Your huddled masses yearning to breathe free,
The wretched refuse of your teeming shore.
Send these, the homeless, tempest-tossed to me,
I lift my lamp beside the golden door!"

As we know, that old cliché doesn't always ring true. There were other obstacles such as a class-conscious society, especially here in New England. However, it was understood that there were opportunities for those willing to apply themselves and to work hard to earn their way into higher life stations. It didn't take Bodenwein long to realize he needed to bury his identity as an immigrant. He learned many lessons outside of elementary school. His formal education ended with the eighth grade in the Groton Public School System. At age 13, he and his family then moved to New London. Young Bodenwein realized he needed to go to work to help support his family -- not unusual for those times. He became a clerk in his father's shoe store.

Shortly after the family moved to New London, Theodore Bodenwein met a man by the name of George E. Starr, who introduced him to a new profession -- commercial printing. In 1844, Starr held a management position in the local newspaper, which came to be known as the Daily Starr, one of New London's first newspapers. Bodenwein learned a great deal from Starr and realized the versatility of gathering information and reporting on it by printing it on a press. He also learned how to set the type tiles manually for the news to be printed – no computers in those days. Consequently, at the age of 17, he developed his own one-page weekly paper titled *The Thames Budget*. The printing was done late at night. With Bodenwein's enthusiasm and exuberance, he would then hawk this one-page paper at his father's shoe shop, enticing curious customers to get the latest news fit to print.

As he continued learning the intricacies of the newspaper business, he was like a fresh sponge, soaking up the local history and the world around him. He also was intrigued by how far-reaching newspapers were. They recorded not only the local news, but that coverage expanded into the regional, as well as the state and national – with no end -- even the international. One could say, by this time, he was hooked; he had newsprint in his veins. He developed a belief that newspapers should not operate just as businesses, but they should champion the rights of all and promote the common good. While he was acquiring this belief, The New London Day was born July 2, 1881. He was learning much of his craft from the publishers, reporters, and printers there.

In 1891, at age 27, Bodenwein's acquired wealth of knowledge and confidence gave him the courage and fortitude to purchase The New London Day Newspaper. I believe he took to heart Thomas Jefferson's infamous quote, when the latter was a delegate to the Continental Congress 1786-88, on the importance of free press:

"... The way to prevent these irregular interpositions of the people is to give them full information of their affairs thro' the channel of public papers, & to contrive that those papers should penetrate the whole mass of the people. The basis of our governments being the opinion of the people, the very first object should be to keep that right; and were it left to me to decide whether we should have a government without newspapers or newspapers without a government, I should not hesitate a moment to prefer the latter. But I should mean that every man should receive those papers & be capable of reading them."

***

For the next forty-eight years, as the publisher of The New London Day, Bodenwein engendered a faithful relationship between newspaper and community. His strongly held beliefs regarding government and community rang out in editorials, outlining much-needed improvements in municipal services. Bodenwein's newspaper provided strong civic leadership. Through his civic involvement over the decades, the improvements flourished as communities were enhanced by the creation of parks, schools, the United States Coast Guard Academy, the U. S. Naval Base, and Connecticut College for Women.

Between Bodenwein and his staff, they braved the elements of bad weather, as well as devastating times of poverty and misery through the Great Depression of 1929, to produce editions without fail. The newspaper struggled financially but managed to survive. If you have ever seen the movie "Grapes of Wrath," or read the heartbreaking novel by John Steinbeck of a family picking up roots, packing the little they then owned, moved across country in their rickety old jalopy of a truck -- an arduous and daunting trip to say the least -- from Oklahoma to California, only to find there were no jobs there either. That will help you visualize precisely what it was like living through the Great Depression.

For the full Day's newspaper history, I encourage you to read: The Day Paper -- *The Story of One of America's Last Independent Newspapers,* written by Gregory N. Stone, printed by The Day Publishing Company and copyrighted 2000. Today, in this age of digital media, The Day once again struggles to survive while maintaining its independence as it continues to give back to the community.

I am reminded of the wonderful movie, *Seabiscuit.* The setting for it started with the famous Great Depression. It showed firsthand the impact and devastation of the American people during that horrendous period. Watching it, one recognizes what the survivors had to endure. These were proud and educated people with well-established careers, which, in a blink of an eye went down the tubes. They found themselves just sitting there, broken in defeat, wondering "what happened?" They struggled to maintain their dignity and their determination to prevail. In the meantime, they were attempting to bolster each other through love and respect from the heart.

I believe it is so important to maintain one's dignity, no matter the circumstances: loss of job, loss of family members, illness, and, of course, the inevitable aging process, which can reduce us to such an undignified state. Maintaining one's dignity and grace is not as easily done, as saying so.

***

In October, 1938, while on his death-bed in New London's Lawrence + Memorial Hospital, Theodore Bodenwein signed his own Will, on which he'd been working with his attorney all that summer. He was concerned about the continuation of The New London Day newspaper. Here's a man who loved this newspaper more than his own life. He saw it as the *people's paper*. Consequently, he had a vision; rather than trusting its management exclusively to his family, he created The Day Trust by appointing five independent trustees to oversee and to manage its affairs. He then transferred ownership of The New London Day to his newly created trust entity. This transfer was unique in that the newspaper was for-profit and The Day Trust was *non-profit, benefiting the*

51

community. The Day, as it is now known, is the only for-profit independent newspaper in the country which is actually *owned by a non-profit trust.*

Under Theodore's Will, the Bodenwein Public Benevolent Foundation was created to provide grants to non-profit organizations. This foundation receives the net proceeds from The Day and disburses those profits to charitable organizations within its circulation. Examples of such grants provide funds for performing arts, social welfare services, environmental protection, education, historic preservation, and libraries. To obtain grants, a charitable non-profit -- *recognized as such by the Internal Revenue Service as a 501(C)(3) entity -- must complete a grant application and submit it to the Bodenwein Public Benevolent Foundation prior to its annual deadline.* A designated distributions committee then reviews all of the applications and makes the decisions.

The newspaper publishes an annual list of charitable organizations chosen as grant recipients.

***

My regret is that I never got to know Mr. Bodenwein. I do so admire him and all that he accomplished, topping it off by the creation of the permanent foundation that continues benefitting those less fortunate, as well as all of the charitable missions. Bodenwein definitely had a soft spot in his heart for folks who are on the street in need of shelter and a hot meal. No doubt he recalled his youth, when at the age of thirteen, he left school and went to work to help his family. He was grateful to learn a trade and to pull himself up by the proverbial boot straps from the working poor.

***

We now move on to a brief history of the creation of the Frank Loomis Palmer Fund. Frank Loomis Palmer was born in June, 1851 to a family with long-established lines in America. Palmer Brothers Company had establishments in several communities within New London County. Their goal was to produce quality, upscale bedding, and accessories for consumers across the country.

As a young entrepreneur in the late 1800s, Frank Loomis Palmer invented a quilting device that greatly increased production of "bed comfortable" quilts and accessories. Given New England's winter climate, this made him quite prosperous. Prior to his invention, quilts had been made painstakingly by hand with tiny, evenly-spaced stitches. Palmer's invention streamlined the process, making it beneficial to the production and easier on the hands and backs of its employees.

If you have ever been to Lancaster County, Pennsylvania, which is known for its exquisite quilts and crafts, you'll know it has been recognized as America's quilt capital. Amish women in Pennsylvania Dutch Country have been creating masterpieces since at least the mid-1800s. Quilts were born partially out of frugality – all through that very process -- and were used as blankets. Today, these artisans not only make quilts but placemats, tea cozies, and other treasures. My sister and I made multiple trips to that area and purchased two of those gorgeous handtied quilts – one king-sized double wedding ring pattern, and the other queen-sized log cabin pattern. These beautiful works of art, created by masters of their craft, earned their title of *masterpieces*.

Over the years, I've been made aware that the process of quilting, basket-weaving, and sewing serves a creative means for socializing, solving problems, and entertainment; not only for the Amish women and girls, but for people all around the world. These gatherings are called *bees* – a social affair where people also work in competitions such as spelling bees. Quilters around the globe specialize in creating these spectacular pieces of art, often denoting a particular theme; such as celebrating an individual's birth, marriage, retirement, patriotism, holidays and, of course, coordinating favorite colors and patterns by artisans telling their stories. To attend one of their quilting shows is an education unto itself.

While I've done a lot of sewing over the years, as well as knitting, rug hooking, and embroidery, I've never done any quilting. I do admire the works of others.

***

Frank Loomis Palmer, had a strong sense of civic duty. In addition to becoming a prominent businessman and continuing his ancestral roots, he served as President of the Savings Bank of New London and as a director of the National Bank of Commerce: the latter having merged into Bank of America. The Savings Bank of New London became the New England Savings Bank and was located in the iconic "Milford Pink" granite building, built in 1852, on what was then Main Street; now Eugene O'Neill Drive. The façade is slightly curved to conform to the bend in the street. Unfortunately, that bank was deactivated in 1993.

In 1917, Palmer died leaving a multi-million-dollar estate to his two daughters: Theodora, born 1882 and Virginia, born 1884. Included in his estate was a magnificent collection of rare 18th century furniture that was deemed "works of art." Furniture from that era was influenced by the French. Today we would refer to them as gorgeous museum pieces, as all were ornate with lots of gold filigree decoration.

In addition to leaving his estate to his daughters, Palmer had instilled in them his own strong sense of civic duty. His daughters treasured their father's memory. In fact, Virginia indicated that her sister and she had always considered the possession of their wealth as joint with their parents, Frank Loomis Palmer and Louisa Townsend Palmer.

In 1934, Virginia Palmer drew up her Last Will and Testament in which she stipulated the donation of several hundred thousand dollars each to such organizations as the Lawrence + Memorial Hospital, Connecticut College for Women, and the Lyman Allyn Art Museum. (Note: the museum was established by a bequest from Harriet Upson Allyn in memory of her father: Captain Lyman Allyn – 1797-1874 – who commanded a whaling ship at the age of twenty-one.) While Palmer was not one of the founding trustees of Connecticut College for Women -- which was chartered by the Connecticut legislature on April 5, 1911 -- he did serve the college as a trustee. Consequently, Virginia's bequest to Connecticut College in his memory became the creation of the over 1200 seat Frank Loomis Palmer Auditorium built in 1939. Unfortunately, Theodora and Virginia were of college age prior to the school's being chartered.

(An interesting side note: the architect for Palmer Auditorium was Shreve, Lamb, and Harmon, the same firm that designed the Empire State Building. Similar to that New York landmark, this auditorium contains art deco features in its stonework as well.)

In her estate plan, Virginia outlined the creation of a trust whose funds were to be distributed: "To corporations, organizations, societies, institutions and trusts located or operating in the City of New London, Connecticut, which are devoted exclusively to religious, charitable, scientific, literary, historical or educational purposes..."

Virginia Palmer died in July 1936. In 1940, the first grants from the Frank Loomis Palmer Fund were made available and continue to this day, awarding charitable non-profit organizations within the City of New London.

***

These two trusts – Bodenwein Public Benevolent Foundation and Frank Loomis Palmer Fund -- were my introduction to charitable trusts and all the good they can do. Each shows ways of giving back to the community and how far-reaching their benefits are. Being philanthropically inclined, one never knows how many thousands of lives are impacted by these generous donors shared love for their neighbors through their thoughtful contributions.

Another type of irrevocable trust is a *Special / Supplemental /Discretionary Needs Trust.* These trusts are created as additions to the federal or state benefits an individual receives for basic needs. Beneficiaries are provided those *extras* that individuals need for bettering the quality of their lives. These supplemental needs might include traveling to see family or providing entertainment or assisting with hobbies.

In addition to establishing private foundations, charitable remainder trusts may be created for one's own benefit or for the benefit of a spouse or another person. There are basically two types of these trusts – *fixed* versus *variable* annuity:

1. Beneficiaries receive *fixed annuities* for life, based on the initial value of funding for that trust. Upon the demise of a beneficiary, the balance goes to a designated charity.

2. The u*ni-trust* establishes the percentage to be paid to the beneficiary. The market value of the trust's assets is determined annually on December 31st. It establishes the amount to be paid to the beneficiary for the next year; consequently, making it a variable rather than a fixed annuity. The advantage to this kind of trust lies in the annual payment to the beneficiary being adjusted each year based on the stock market value of the trust's assets. If

the stock market's value is higher the next year, one receives an increase in the annual payment.

However, the reverse is also true. If the stock market is lower the following year, then the annual payment decreases for that forthcoming period. In determining which type of trust is best for the beneficiary, one must consider the other resources available.

I share these brief definitions of the various kinds of trusts available for use in families. Obviously, one's own personal situation should be addressed with an attorney who is familiar with the estate planning process. Oh yes, don't forget to mention to your estate planner if you have a pet and what is to become of it after your death. *Yes, you can actually set up a trust for the benefit of your pet's continuing happy life.*

Chapter 4

My Career Continues

At the time I joined the trust department of Hartford National Bank & Trust Company, there were four officers and four secretaries. Because of all of the legal work involved and the need to read and understand the various documents, some trust officers were also lawyers; that practice continues today.

I served as a secretary there for about a year, when I had an offer for another job. As I indicated, there were four secretaries in our department. While I loved the business to which I had been exposed and found it a valuable learning experience, I was only doing everyone's filing, *or things they just didn't want to do themselves.* As an example, I had to type, verbatim, wills and trust agreements onto stencils for mimeographing. (Those of you attending schools between the 1950s and 1970s must remember those moments when the teacher distributed copies of tests or work sheets with the heady glue-like pungent aroma and distinct purple ink referred to as "dittos.")

The type of mimeographing machines used by businesses were huge ones requiring stencils to be cut by typing. The stencils then needed to be wrapped and fastened around a cylinder. Rotating the cylinder forced the ink through the stencil and onto individual sheets of paper served up from a tray. At the bank, this machine was governed by a man who also controlled the mail room and other jobs. (Be thankful for today's technology and *don't take it for granted.*)

We didn't have the capabilities at that time for photocopying; or when we did, it was a very wet and often messy process. In order to pour the liquid into the machine, it would sometimes spill or splatter onto one's clothing, ruining an entire outfit.

One could not take legal documents apart for copying for a couple of reasons. These were *original* documents. If you took them apart, someone could easily slip an unauthorized page into it and change the disposition of the estate by substituting names *unrelated to the decedent*. Usually, these originals were very impressive with their official seals, comprised of ribbons and wax. If you've ever had a document notarized, the notary uses a small hand-held machine to press a seal into the paper. This process is called *embossing*. Today, one occasionally finds a bank using its corporate seal, or there are foil seals added to diplomas, degrees, and official documents. (Again, don't take modern technology for granted!)

Since I was taking courses through the American Institute of Banking, I knew that the bank offered continuing education. When this other job opportunity came up, I decided to talk with "The Boss" Clark Moseley, who scared me half to death with his austere gruff voice and treasure trove of knowledge. Of course, he was considerably older than me. I was twenty-three, naïve, and inexperienced in the working world. I must say, though, when I really got to know Mr. Moseley, he became the most wonderful mentor to me. For those of you who have seen the movie, "The

Karate Kid," you'll remember Mr. 'Miagi' (Pat Morita): a sage older *gentleman serving as a custodian* in the apartment building where *The Kid* and his mom had moved. Mr. Miagi, as you may recall, was the Karate Master. Mr. Moseley was that kind of a mentor to me. He would patiently explain things and plant seeds for me to mull over and adapt as appropriate.

I remember so well going to him and asking if I could meet with him in private, to which he agreed. When we were in the bank's library, which doubled as a conference room, I addressed him as Mr. Moseley and informed him that I had *not gone on to school merely to become a filing clerk.* I boldly let him know I needed to apply practical use of my secretarial skills if I were to be efficient in my position; I was afraid those skills would diminish over time due to a lack of application. I also shared with him that I had an offer from a law firm where my capabilities might be more appreciated. I explained to him that I liked working for Hartford National Bank. I found this to be a truly vexing challenge --

deciding whether to stay with the bank, or to take that offered position with the law firm.

We discussed various opportunities available within the bank versus my going to work for the law firm. He assured me, if I decided to stay, he would personally see to it that I had an opportunity to use my previously acquired skills. And that is precisely what we did.

***

Mr. Moseley's secretary went on vacation for two weeks. At that time in banking, all officers and employees must annually take two consecutive weeks off for security reasons. (The bank auditors were looking for any possible embezzlement, the set-up of fake bank accounts, money laundering, and other possible scams.) He asked me to fill in for her, which I did.

I lost ten pounds in the first week. No exaggeration. The minute he spoke, I was on the move to get whatever he needed -- whether it was a file from downstairs, typing letters from his dictations, and other related duties. After his secretary's vacation, he had me fill in for all of the others during their time off.

***

In addition to administering a wide variety of trusts, these departments also settle estates of decedents ... those who have passed on. Under the decedent's will, an executor is appointed by the Probate Court for the district in which the deceased individual had resided. The executor is responsible for collecting, identifying, and establishing <u>fair market values</u> for all of the deceased's assets. The executor must then file a detailed inventory of those assets with the Court.

Usually, if there are no surviving family members locally, as in this case, the executor is responsible for cleaning out the home. The boss had me join him and his secretary with a certain estate ... my very first direct involvement in a decedent's assets. In this particular estate there was a large, three-story family summer home right on Long Island Sound. The home also included three stories of servants' quarters. In this case, the deceased was a single lady and the end of her family line. The summer home was fully furnished with gorgeous antiques. This was an opportunity for my eyes to be opened, not only with the fabulous antiques -- about which Mr. Moseley would tell me -- but I also learned that one did not attempt to accumulate *stuff*.

Among these impressive antiques was a magnificent grandfather's clock lording over the staircase landing. Its chimes contained the deepest, most mellow tone, as it musically proclaimed the time. It had to have been a family heirloom. Mr. Moseley went into detail with me regarding the inner wooden-gear workings of that particular grandfather's clock. It was fascinating. This particular clock was definitely an antique; but how old it was in the mid-1960s, I don't know. I will tell you that in 1656, a Dutchman named Christian Huygens was the first person to use a pendulum as a mechanism for creating accurate ticking in clocks. This was the birth of the Grandfather Clock, or to use the proper terminology: Long Case Clock.

When I was mesmerized by Mr. Moseley's description of the inner workings of that gorgeous long case clock, I became fascinated with the antique clocks. The first long case clocks were produced in Britain, after the London clock maker, Ahasurerus Fromenteel, sent his son to Holland to learn about the use of a pendulum. For the first fifteen years, Long Case clock makers struggled to develop a pendulum capable of keeping accurate time. By 1670, an anchor escapement had been developed, which, when used in conjunction with a pendulum, allowed greater accuracy to be achieved. In addition, the weights were installed with *pulley devices* that were coordinated with the accurate time mechanism to sound the chimes at certain intervals – on the hour and half hour, with some clocks even striking on the quarter-hour.

For example, when my parents retired in 1970, they each received a cash gift, which they pooled and used for buying a smaller version of the Grandfather's Clock called ... the *Grandmother's* Clock. Our clock needed to be wound every eight days; it chimes the time on the hour plus every fifteen minutes.

That nearly half-century old clock still graces our living room, chiming perfect time to this day.

The earliest cases for these beautiful time instruments were made from oak and were architectural in appearance. Higher quality clocks would be finished with ebony or pearwood; later cases were made from high quality African mahogany.

It was truly a magnificent heirloom!

***

In cleaning out the rooms, Mr. Moseley told me what to look for and what to throw into a corner that would go to the dump. I went to work on the lady's second-floor bedroom and closet. Mind you, the house was an old summer home with no lights in the closets. The bedroom wasn't bad but the closet was full of shelves. Those shelves were full of *stuff,* including trinkets, books, and photo albums. It appeared she had been given gifts that were barely out of their wrapping paper. Obviously, the decedent had just set these unused items on the shelves, often in their original

70

wrappings, but opened. On the closet floor there were boxes full of more stuff: fabric remnants, old clothing patterns, receipts, miscellaneous papers, little trinkets; quite a mixture of basic rubbish.

Clearing the shelves was not a problem, but my imagination was getting going about what I might find in those full boxes on the floor of this dark closet that contained no natural or artificial illumination. *Would I find a rat?* I had experienced plenty of those creepy rodents while living in that efficiency apartment in Boston. Possibly I'd find a snake curled up in a dark corner, and ready to strike? Even though this was the second floor – *snakes do climb.*

And of course, there were always those intrepid little rodents that love dark corners of attics: mice. Those tiny varmints are capable of snuggling into the softest, most desirable nesting places. Perhaps, while sitting comfortably in one of those nice soft chairs, I'd discover a mother mouse with her suckling babies there too.

I knew that most of a particular box's contents would go in the *dump corner*. I was going right along; but as I tossed an item into the corner, my eye caught something amiss. Had something moved in that box? I blinked -- telling myself to stop imagining things. But the next time I reached gingerly into the box, I fixed my eyes on its contents and not in the direction of the corner where I was tossing things.

Nothing moved.

About that time, Mr. Moseley came to the doorway and asked in his gruff voice: "How's everything going in here, Millie?"

My response: "Oh, just fine, Mr. Moseley, but I think there might be a mouse or something in this box."

His reply, "Well ... just take it out!"

I was aghast at the mere thought of having to handle whatever it was, which caused me to immediately reply, "Not me, Mr. Moseley, YOU!" Yes, as I said it, I was even pointing my finger at him.

72

Needless to say, I was grateful that he didn't go macho on me but became fatherly as he recognized the fear coming over me and came to my defense by taking care of it himself. He checked the box and the next fabric remnant to be removed uncovered mother mouse with her tiny nursing babies. I learned then and there that the big, tough, austere Mr. Moseley with his gruff voice was a sensitive, caring, and humane individual. He promptly picked up the box, carried it downstairs, setting it carefully outside the door. By the time we went to lunch, 'Mama Mouse' and her babies had all gone off on their merry mouse ways.

From that time on, every time I'd go to the Supply Closet in our office, Mr. Moseley would say, "Look out, Millie, there may be a mouse!"

At the holiday time in the office, we always had a Christmas tree in the bowed window and each year we would draw names for gifts. The price was set for each of our gifts at *one dollar*, and wouldn't you know it, I drew Mr. Moseley's name! Well, now I was feeling the stress. What does one buy for The Boss that costs a *dollar*? I racked my brain, thinking and thinking; and then the light dawned.

My gift would have to have a mouse theme.

My sister and I drove over to Groton, just across the Gold Star Memorial Bridge (before its inclusion in the I-95 corridor when a second bridge was added), to a very small holiday gift shop. I told the owner what I was looking for, the price, and why. She was wonderful. She came out with a tiny round cellulose box with replicas of Mama Mouse and her babies. Each was made out of wood, with little beady eyes, leather ears, and long tails also made of leather -- all for $1.00.

I was ecstatic!

We came home, found a large box with lots of tissue paper. I lifted out half of the paper, set the tiny package of mice in the center. I made sure they were totally covered, and wrapped it in the most angelic paper with a huge bow. As was our custom, I put his name on the package; but didn't sign the gift tag. I then took the gift into the office, and placed it under the tree when Mr. Moseley was out of the office.

Well, I discovered the *little child* within Mr. Moseley. He spotted the gift had been added under the tree, which was next to his desk. Lo and behold, he discovered it had his name on it. He'd pick it up, shake it, and then put it back. When it came time for all of us to open the gifts, as he opened his and lifted out half of the paper, he found Mama Mouse and babies. He exclaimed with a big smile and twinkle in his eyes: "I don't have to guess who this is from; I know!" We all had a good laugh. He was really just a *big kid.* It was then I discovered that he was a true artist who enjoyed wood carving. In fact, his degree had been in art. I was very touched a number of years later, when in conversation with Mr. Moseley, he let me know that he still had the mama mouse and babies that I'd given him.

Following the exchange of gifts, I began to relax around The Boss. As I mentioned, he became the most wonderful mentor to me. As I continued growing in my position at the Bank, I always called him "Mr. Moseley" until some six years later when I was made a Trust Officer. Officers didn't call each other by Mr. or Mrs. I had so much respect for him, it was hard for me to call him by his first name; but I finally did call him *Clark*.

I remember in particular one piece of advice he gave me and that was in the form of a question for me to answer, which I've shared with other dear friends in their moving up their respective ladders: "Do you want to be a little fish in a big pond or a big fish in a little pond?" The answer to that question for me would determine whether I went to Hartford or elsewhere in the state to work, or to stay in New London. I opted to stay in New London. And I am so glad that I did. Again, I believe the decision was part of the Lord's Plan.

CHAPTER 5

Ongoing Life Changes

Our parents both retired in June, 1970. During the winter of 1971 they took a trip to Florida, for a couple of weeks. In July, all four of us shared a week's vacation in Wells Beach, Maine. It was absolutely delightful. I still remember how cold that water was at Wells Beach, but Pop would run down in the sand and dive into the frigid ocean. I think of it even now and still shiver ... BBBrrrr.

One Monday morning in August over breakfast, we were all talking about the trip we would take the next summer. We were planning that Mom and Pop would drive out west, Katie and I would fly out to join them; then we would tour the national parks together. Katie and I would fly back home; Mom and Pop would continue the balance of the return trip by car.

After breakfast, Katie left around eight o'clock for work in Hartford. About the same time, I left for the bank. Getting into work, I had gone out to the front of the bank to secure information for my assigned project.

Unbeknownst to me, the boss had taken a call from my mother a short while ago. He'd come to find me. His face was ashen -- troubled. He informed me of the call from Mom and that I needed to go to her right away.

While mowing the front lawn, my dad had just *dropped*. He had been taken to the hospital. I was told to pick up Mom and drive her there. When I got home, Mom informed me that Pop had died. I couldn't believe it. I drove her to the hospital where it was confirmed; he had died of a massive heart attack.

He had only just turned 63. What a shock his death was for all of us!

Yes, I had lost other family members and friends; but no one as close as my own father. I was in shock. Devastated. All of us were. It was our faith, family, and friends seeing us through that traumatic period. I still remember vividly the calling hours for him and the three-hundred-plus people – family, friends, co-workers, and others from his past -- who came to offer their condolences. He was a compassionate, caring, and very special person, beloved by so many. As I was growing up, I recall accompanying him to church in downtown New London and his greeting just about everyone with: "Hi, Red!"

I asked him if everyone was really named 'Red.'

He'd chuckle and stated he couldn't remember names; but it was important to recognize people. He had always thought it was the sort of thing that made them feel good. And, to boot, he usually tipped his hat, as well.

Dad's passing in 1971 was my first traumatic experience with death. At 29, I had lost not only my dad, but my best friend and confidant. We were that close.

I'll always remember my dad while growing up and having a dog. To begin with, a few memories come to mind. We had a wonderful mutt named Shadow. Apparently, Mom and Dad had him for a while before I was born. He was inky black. I never asked how old he was when he had died; but I was a very young child. Mom and Dad had a wonderful way with pets, whether our own, someone else's, or a stray … It didn't matter to them, cats or dogs.

***

While I was in junior high and the beginning of high school, we were in the *poodle skirt era.* All of the girls wore poodle skirts to the dances. The skirts had poodle dogs appliquéd on the full skirts. Remember my Loretta Young moment? How I loved dressing up in particularly full skirts that swirled as you danced and spun around, making them flare out.

Speaking of poodles … Oh, how I wanted a poodle for my very own dog. My parents were willing to get one; they would never have said 'no' to a poodle, knowing how much I wanted one of these adorable, precious little pooches. However, one evening while Dad was relaxing comfortably in his favorite, barrel-back upholstered chair, his feet up on the hassock, and reading the evening newspaper, he came across an ad for adorable Samoyed puppies, as opposed to the desired poodle. He showed us a picture of the Samoyed pups. He urged us to go take a look at them. That's all it took – even though my heart had been set on a poodle.

The Samoyed breed belongs to the Husky family. The puppies were newly born and not yet ready to leave their mother. I held one of those adorable little balls of fluffy fur in the palm of my hand. They were all white, furry, with black eyes and black noses. Their little ear tips bent down – so cute and cuddly. We fell in love with every one of them, but there was one special little pup that spoke to me. Who knew he would be a blessing to our home? And to boot, he was *the runt of the litter*.

When the pups reached six weeks old, they were ready for new homes. They were pure-bred and registered with the American

Kennel Club. We went back to pick up my special one that I'd selected; now it took both hands for me to hold this little furry pup against my chest. That puppy would grow to be a medium-sized, thick, long-haired dog, and a very strong *sixty-five-pound*, fabulous pet. He regarded me as a pushover, and how he loved to play … whether with me, or other family members. And how he also loved to frolic in the snow! His breed is trained normally as sled dogs. Think of the movies and TV shows we've seen from the Alaskan frontier with its teams of huskies … *Mush*!

When we went to register him officially with the American Kennel Club, the obvious name Sam was already taken. Debbie Reynolds TAMMY series of movies were ever popular at that time. I loved those movies. Consequently, even though he was definitely a male, we registered him officially as 'Tammy' … but we always called him 'Sam.'

Whenever I stooped down to get something from a lower kitchen cabinet, Sam would put his big paws on my shoulders and pull me down onto the floor with him. Of course, he'd then lap my face until his tongue ran dry.

He would always get so excited when someone came to the front door – even more so, when he would see another dog. Pop was the only one with the strength to control Sam while out walking, especially if another dog came by. Of course, our Samoyed husky was very curious and just had to mark his territory; even though he'd been spayed, he really got excited around female dogs. He would bark, jump around, and tug on his leash. He was such a good-natured dog, always seemed so happy. He was a fabulous pet, and a true family member.

We had him from 1956-1970. Fourteen years is considered a long life, especially for that breed of dog. By that age, they are considered geriatric. While he was a great loss to all of us, because of his closeness to Pop all those years, we were glad he didn't have to experience my dad's sudden heart attack and death.

***

Over the years I have come to realize it is natural and not out of the ordinary to feel distraught over the death of those who were close to me. They are no longer physically with us but one still feels their *presence*. Yes, your life is changed; but those beloved spirits may come back to you in a pet phrase of their own ... or a feeling of being hugged, when no one else is physically there. I even had one of those moments while being alone in my home and walking into my bedroom. There was a pungent scent of Ben Gay, an ointment used to sooth aches and pains. I didn't even own any Ben Gay ... but the memory took me back to my parents and especially to my two dear single aunts, who had lived next door in the old family homestead. You think back over various sentimental, humorous, and just fun times shared; like those beloved days with our dog, Sam, who so enjoyed romping through the snow with Pop.

Another favorite story of mine about my dad -- who was definitely *not* a cook -- was when Mom had made a loaf of gingerbread. It was in the oven baking and, when the timer sounded, *needed* to be removed. Mom asked Pop simply to remove the loaf when the buzzer sounded and place it on the cooling rack. She had to leave to pick up Katie and me from our piano lessons, which were clear across town.

At the buzzing of the timer, Pop followed dutifully her instructions, removing the loaf from the oven. However, as he did so, he remembered that Mom always tested the baked items to be sure they were done before removing them. He had no idea what kind of utensils she used. So, he improvised by grabbing a straw from the broom, ignoring whatever dust it had accumulated, and tested the gingerbread. All seemed well -- until he remembered that Mom also always turned the baked item out of its pan and onto the cooling rack. On this particular occasion, the *hot* gingerbread broke in half! Part of it landed upside down on the cooling rack; the other half remained stuck in the baking dish. He was sure he'd be dreadfully in trouble with Mom due to his … unbelievable mishap.

When we all returned home, my sister Katie was the first one into the house. Dad urgently took her aside and immediately told her what he'd done and what had happened. He was in dire need of her help. He was feeling so guilty over the outcome of his good deeds that had gone awry. Katie went with him to the kitchen to firsthand survey what had happened and to assess what could be done. She became Pop's heroine by putting the half from the cooling rack back into the dish, thereby saving the day. No harm was done and no one was upset; but we all had a good, hardy laugh over this disastrous episode at Pop's expense.

***

What Katie and I discovered, following Pop's sudden passing, was that while he and Mom had been in Florida, she had had medical issues too. These ailments became more pronounced following his death. With Pop's passing and Mom's medical issues … these matters became definitely life-altering for us all.

Katie and I both had Power of Attorney for financial and healthcare for Mom. With Katie's living and working in Hartford and my working in New London, as well as living at home, I would accompany Mom to her doctors' appointments. I did my best to comprehend what these medical professionals were saying. In the mid-1970s she was having perpetual bouts with what we thought was merely laryngitis. Being a kindergarten teacher, especially dealing with sixty children per day, required using her voice an awful lot. She went to see an ears, nose and throat specialist, who diagnosed her symptoms and advised her to be operated on for a paralyzed vocal cord. During the operation they injected a Teflon solution into her paralyzed cord, which made it more stable for the second cord to hit it. It resulted in the normal working of her vocal cords and ended her bouts with laryngitis.

Who would have thought the Teflon brand formula that was created in 1938 by DuPont for coatings in cookware would become so versatile? Today, that special formula, plus additives, is used not only in cookware but in paints, fabrics, carpets, home furnishings, clothing, and so much more. As we discovered in the mid-1970s, it was also used successfully in medical procedures.

I saw her that day following the operation. All seemed fine. The next day, when I went in to see her, however, I could smell that distinct antiseptic hospital odor. I also noticed oxygen masks and tubes at the ready, as well as an oxygen tank in her private room – *items that had not been there the day before.* In chatting with her, Mom told me that she'd "had a problem during the night"; but she wasn't able to offer any particular details. So, I offered to go down to the nurses' station to see if I could get more information.

As it turned out, my mother's primary care doctor was sitting there reviewing charts. I boldly interrupted him and asked him to bring me up to date on the nature of what had transpired during the night regarding my mother. He peered up over his glasses, stood to his full six foot-plus height, throwing his bony shoulders back in arrogant fashion, deliberately towering over me. While inspecting his own finger nails, he proceeded condescendingly into a long explanation, utilizing all of the proper Latin medical terms. He was most impressed with his own knowledge – and clearly his own importance. Of course, I didn't have a clue as to what he'd said – and he knew it – which definitely got *my Irish up.* I let him finish, thanked him politely, then asked him to repeat what he had said in *laymen's terms* so I could understand it. He did so reluctantly, capping it off with an audible sigh.

It seems that Mom had had congestive heart failure during the night, but was now doing okay. It would have been nice if he'd volunteered that information in the first place.

Following that episode I noticed, whenever the hospital provided my mother's meals to her, they were low-salt and not particularly appetizing: bland -- *tasteless.* I think we are all aware of that typical hospital food from years past. Having made that observation, I anticipated, when she was discharged, they would recommend a special diet or at least give her some *guidance.* They did not. So, I called the doctor's office, requesting specific guidelines. I asked … "How would we know if she were having any more heart problems?" His curt answer: "You'll know!" No special diet was offered. In other words: *no guidance at all.*

***

This doctor was especially short on 'bed-side manner.' He, no doubt, might have been better suited for medical work behind the scenes, such as research. Anywhere that did not involve direct contact with patients and their families. He definitely was not a 'Marcus Welby', M.D. (Robert Young) from the delightful and informative 1969-76 TV series -- a doctor who even made warm and kindly house-calls.

***

Since long before Pop died, we, as a family, had already gone to a low-salt diet and used other spices and seasonings to stimulate the palate. After his passing, we focused more on chicken, fish, and other healthier proteins and ingredients, rather than the heavier, more fatty meat products; such as bacon, beef, pork, and others.

If my sister Katie or I ever brought up the topic of Pop's passing to our mother, she would listen; but our mother never brought up anything to do with him, even with us, her own daughters. Mom was never one to share her own feelings. She was so stoic.

In 1978, Mom was home alone during the day. Katie was at work in Hartford; I was working in New London, but doing a fair amount of traveling for the bank. One day around noon, as Katie often did, she called Mom from Hartford. Mom expressed concern due to her stomach acting up. She thought an Alka-Seltzer and some rest would help. From what Mom had said, Katie sensed this was not a normal upset stomach. Mom had never been one to complain about ailments; she had always been a very private person. Katie suspected this was not the norm. She tried remaining calm, so not to alarm Mom. But all kinds of thoughts were running through my sister's mind. She told Mom she would call her back in a half hour. Fortunately, she did just that.

With Katie's natural inquisitive nature – she began thinking and worrying: was this *the dreaded sign* we should recognize with the return of the congestive heart failure? With the second call, she knew something definitely was wrong.

It was much more than a normal stomach ache. Mom was having trouble breathing and she felt a tightness in her chest. Katie tried to reach me at the bank; but I was in an official bank meeting. She didn't interrupt me, nor leave a message. Instead, she called our dear cousin, Gertrude, who was about to go grocery shopping with her dad, but said they'd come right over.

Fortunately, United Parcel Service had delivered a package that morning, which Mom had taken. In closing the front door, which locks automatically, she didn't quite shut it all the way. The door had not latched; consequently, allowing our cousin Gertrude and her dad to let themselves into our home. Immediately they saw Mom, whose lips were turning blue. Gertrude called me and I called 9-1-1. The operator was wonderful. She kept me on the line to keep me informed.

The Waterford Ambulance, located at the Quaker Hill Fire Company, is about a mile from our home. The 911 emergency operator told me that in spite of Mom's doctor being in Norwich

-- who would meet her at the Backus Hospital -- it was quicker for the ambulance to take her to Lawrence + Memorial Hospital in New London. She would confirm with the ambulance driver once the emergency team had assessed the situation, as to which hospital they'd be taking her.

While waiting on the phone, -- to me it seemed like an eternity -- I told the operator that I was only four miles from home; perhaps I could get there while they were attending her. She said "Okay," but to call back if I missed them. She would let me know where they took her.

I arrived home just as the ambulance was backing out of our driveway. I could see they were headed toward New London. I pulled my car over to the side of the road, jumped out, hailed them, and hustled into the ambulance. When we got to the hospital, I went to the pay phones, called Katie, filled her in; then called our home -- mind you this was all *well before cell phones*. I talked with Gertrude and confirmed with her to bring Mom's handbag, containing her medical cards, which she did. Of course, there was a little confusion in between our conversations. A rather important detail was missing in my instructions: Gertrude went to Backus Hospital in Norwich and, of course, we were at Lawrence + Memorial in New London. I felt so badly when I realized I'd forgotten to tell her about the switch in hospitals. I had to call her at the emergency room of Backus to have her come from Norwich to New London, approximately a thirty-minute drive.

After calling Gertrude, I called Mom's primary care physician to let him know she had been taken to Lawrence + Memorial Hospital due to its being closer. His immediate response was, "It wouldn't have taken much longer to bring her to Backus." My response was: "No, only the difference between life and death."

Needless to say, after that incident we changed doctors.

We came so close to losing Mom that day, but the good Lord was with us. Apparently, He wasn't quite ready to take her home with Him. It was touch and go for a couple of days, but she came through it like the proverbial trooper.

***

From that day on, we made sure that Mom was never left alone. We hired a companion, who was with her 8:00 A.M. until 5:00 P.M., Monday through Friday. I cared for Mom at home, when I wasn't working; oversaw her diet, and the rest of her day-to-day needs. She was frequently hooked up to oxygen; consequently, no one was permitted to smoke in our home.

My dear cousin, Gertrude Minson, was a fourth-grade teacher in Montville. Whenever I knew I'd be late getting home, she would bring her students' papers over to correct while at our home and relieving the companion at 5:00 P.M. She would stay with Mom until I eventually arrived home. God bless Gertrude. She would be with my mom while I was finishing up at work, or at a board meeting such as Family Services, where we were dealing with the new executive director.

I was very grateful to Katie and her ongoing inquiring mind. Whenever Mom had doctors' appointments, I was always armed with questions. Once home from appointments, I'd call Katie and gave her all of the answers I'd obtained. Of course, by then she'd come up with at least twenty more. They were always good questions, but I was also very frustrated, feeling I too should have asked more questions. It was during that stressful period when I learned one of life's greatest lessons: one should never second guess oneself. It does absolutely no good.

Mom remained mostly at home following that episode. It lasted approximately three-and-a-half years until one day, when we knew she wasn't getting enough oxygen, or that *something was wrong*. We knew she wanted to be at home rather than being placed in a nursing home. It was a Saturday. Katie called the Emergency Room of Lawrence + Memorial Hospital and spoke with a wonderful, compassionate doctor who asked Katie if Mom had been declared incompetent or incapable of handling her own affairs. Her answer was a resounding "No!" The doctor told her in that case it was *not* our decision to make. It was Mom's. He also made it clear that *we should* ask her and then abide by her decision. We asked her whether she wanted to go to the hospital or stay at home. She said she definitely needed to go to the hospital.

As it turned out, she was in the hospital that time for four weeks; then a nursing home for four more. Mom died there in November, 1982. And through our own faith, we knew our parents had been reunited in heaven.

***

Earlier in this chapter, I shared with you how devastated I was in the loss of my dear father. Katie was as close to Mom as I was to Pop, and she was truly devastated by Mom's death. Fortunately, she sought counseling, which helped her in dealing with the magnitude of her loss.

In hindsight, I've realized that Katie's temperament was very similar to Pop's; while mine was much like Mom's. As they say: opposites do attract.

Time does have a way of healing. Over the years, considering that the loss of one parent came with no warning, while the other passed away after a long illness, we came to the following conclusion: while it is very difficult to lose a loved one abruptly, you still remember that individual as having been very much alive. It is quite a different thing to watch a loved one struggling through the lengthy illness. That memory also stays with you.

I will never forget the wonderful tenor soloist, Don Hawkins, who sang at Mom's funeral. One of the beautiful hymns he performed was *In the Garden* by C. Austin Miles. That particular hymn has a very lively refrain that Don invited us all to join in on.

> "And He walks with me, and He talks with me,
> And He tells me I am His own,
> And the joy we share as we tarry there …
> None other has ever known."

That hymn was particularly uplifting to me, especially when everyone joined in.

***

From high school on, I had male friends through a variety of experiences. I always thought I would marry and have a family; however, that just didn't work out for me. While I was caring for our mom, working full-time, and serving as president of a non-profit board, one such friend told me I had given up my life for my mother. Well, that ended my relationship with him. Later, another male friend, with whom I thought I had a good, loving relationship, telephoned me two days before a bank-sponsored black-tie event to inform me that I was too public a figure. The truth is he just couldn't deal with it. But at least I was glad that he had been honest with me. Needless to say, that left me picking up the pieces of yet another broken relationship, and scrambling to find an escort for that Saturday night black-tie event.

Another man insisted I should be getting paid for all of my volunteer work. I know opposites attract but this was beyond 'opposites'; it was downright adversarial. Obviously, he didn't know me, nor had he ever met anyone else in my family. Our mom and dad, as well as our aunts, were very well known within southeastern Connecticut. One couldn't go anywhere with them without running into somebody they knew.

Following that memorable black-tie event, our regional senior bank manager suggested that I not worry about having a date for these affairs, but to bring my sister instead. Consequently, my sister got to enjoy a number of those events with me. My stress level went down considerably, as well as my blood pressure.

I think back over relationships. Some were too confining, with a man always trying to control me. It made me feel claustrophobic to say the least. As I look back on having dealt with such relationships, a single thought always runs through my mind: *"Butterflies are free and so must I be!"*

Chapter 6

Building Career in the 1970s and 1980s

Mom and her sisters lived by their favorite saying: "Let me live in a house by the side of the road and be a friend to mankind." My dear two single aunts were teachers and community minded. Therefore, being involved in the community is deeply ingrained in me. My sister Katie and I were involved in various aspects of the community; hence, as our family decreased in size, the *Community* became our family.

I have served on numerous non-profit boards -- and as president of many over the years, as well as business and professional organizations -- which all started when I was in high school.

When I went off to Boston to the Cambridge School of Business and started working through their one-year executive secretarial work-study program, where I had to take the "T" to work from class, I did not make time to get involved. Thus, for that year I wasn't involved in any extra-curricular activities.

That would come home to haunt me, just prior to graduation.

I was told there were two of us eligible to be valedictorian of our class; but ... they were not choosing me, because *I had not been involved in extra-curricular activities*. Wow! I was stunned; especially since I'd been so active throughout high school. But ... they were right. I hadn't made time in my schedule to be involved in the school, nor with my classmates.

Once I was working full-time for Hubbs Engine Company, I spoke with our woman office manager, who provided me with information on The Proparvulis Club, a non-profit Catholic-based organization. I joined the all-women club whose mission was to raise money to get inner-city-underprivileged children out of the city of Boston, and to summer camp at Sunset Point in Hull, Massachusetts. The club's motto: "Having Fun Doing Good."

My getting involved was my real initiation and indoctrination into the not-for-profit world of fund-raising. In particular, I remember the wonderful fashion shows we women would sponsor, in which we were often the models. Sometimes we would have to walk the runway, as professional models do, while showing off the clothing we were enticing our audience of women to purchase. Other times we roamed among the luncheon tables of ladies while the moderator described the special outfit we were sporting.

Fundraising continued back in Connecticut through the Norwich-New London National Secretaries Association Chapter, which included fashion shows, where once again we served as models to an all-female audience. The clothes we modeled were from a local women's clothing store. Of course, we usually were encouraged to buy the clothing we wore for those shows. Naturally, we were always told how nice the outfits looked on us, or how they brought out the color of our eyes. These were definitely sales women doing their jobs – selling.

I was also editor and publisher of the STENOSCOPE, printed on dittos (remember that pungent odor with the purple ink), the chapter's monthly publication for members. In it, I was creative with my typewriter in drawing pictures such as the details of a manual typewriter, including its platen roller that controlled the paper, the carriage that manually had to be returned to the right side for typing the next line of text, typewriter keys, and so forth.

Believe me, computers are a most welcomed electronic benefit to the business world replacing those manual typewriters!

***

From the day I started working as a secretary for Hartford National Bank and Trust Company, I was involved in chairing the Women's Committee for our chapter of the American Institute of Banking. Our role was to provide social events for the chapter. One such event I chaired was a ski trip to Gore Mountain in North Creek, New York. Mind you, I knew *nothing* about skiing, but it sounded like great fun and was sure to be an adventure. Due to my organizing and coordinating the trip through the tour company, it provided me with an unexpected bonus: the tour company paid all my expenses, including free ski lesson.

It was indeed quite the adventure. If memory serves me right, we stayed in the Saratoga Springs, New York area, which was approximately a thirty-to-forty-minute drive to the base of the mountain. Unfortunately, due to the outside temperature being *twenty below zero*, our diesel-powered bus froze up overnight; consequently, once the mechanic and driver got the bus going, there was no heat at all for the trip to the mountain base.

By the time we reached Gore Mountain, not only were we shivering, and our teeth chattering, but I, for one, felt like my face was going to slide off. Think about being on a bus for over a half-hour with no heat in those frigid temperatures. Just recalling it makes me shiver. So, upon arrival at the mountain, many of us scurried into the lodge and warmed up before even considering taking ski lessons in that bitter cold. Of course, there were those hardy souls more accustomed to such harsh weather, who immediately dashed off the bus and headed to the ski slopes.

Once warmed up again, we ventured out to where the lessons would start and began learning the basics. This entailed using rental equipment and, of course, not being fully knowledgeable about securing the skis to the boots, I ran into a major problem. As I was preparing to glide down the beginners' hill, often referred to as the *bunny slope*, one of my skis popped off and went flying down the slope to the bottom. I trudged down that hill in the snow to retrieve it. And I discovered just how icy it was. Since I like having all of my bones intact, I promptly put my skis in the rack and said "enough already." I retreated, once again, to the nice warm lodge with that blazing fire roaring away before me. A nice cup of delicious hot chocolate was warranted at that point, welcomed, and enjoyed. Of course, those of drinking age ordered hot toddies consisting of the following ingredients:

1 teaspoon of honey
2 fluid ounces of boiling water
1 ½ fluid ounces of whiskey or bourbon

3 whole cloves
1 cinnamon stick
1 slice of lemon
1 pinch of ground nutmeg

A truly warming, and delightfully yummy drink ... for those of age!

The next day several of us decided that we'd had enough skiing and opted instead for a sleigh ride at the top of the mountain. We had to take the open chairlift to the summit in the sub-zero, crystal clear, frigid weather.

What do you envision when you hear *sleigh ride?* No doubt, similar thoughts came to you as they did to us. We thought this sleigh ride would be a traditional sleigh, containing warm lap robes, and led by a team of beautiful horses. When we reached the top of the mountain, our dreams were shattered as we saw our so-called sleigh. It was actually a makeshift, loosely constructed sled ... more akin to a cardboard box. But at least it was built on iron runners. No gorgeous horses pulling our sleigh, no classy paint job, no elegant designs ... nothing of that romantic sort. Our horsepower was provided by a *tractor*. Oh yes, and there were a few pieces of straw thrown on the floor of this so-called sleigh, probably the lodge's idea *of ambiance*.

Our ride began and the scenery was magnificent: birds chirping cheerfully, and brilliant sunshine, but it was bitter cold – a bright sun but no warmth. All of a sudden, our peaceful, serene, and glorious ride turned ugly, as we rounded a steep curve, and the sleigh tipped over with all thirty of us piled on top of one another. We were shocked!

We had no advance warning that conditions were so bad! Obviously, neither the lodge nor the driver were aware of the iciness. The driver sallied on totally in his own little world, oblivious to our plight. Come on, we were completely flipped over and lost. Consequently, we were dragged for some distance across that rough icy snow. When he realized ultimately what had happened, he finally stopped. While taking our time, each of us struggled to crawl out from underneath the overturned sleigh, and checked for injuries. Fortunately, aside from scrapes, bumps, bruises, and some blood … no one was seriously hurt. Thank God! To say the least, we were all shaken by this unfortunate incident.

And by the way, with absolutely no assistance from the dolt of a driver, we passengers were the ones who righted the sleigh. Once it was upright on its runners, we climbed reluctantly aboard, once again, while dreading the stability of our ride back to the mountain top. We were all chattering about what alternatives we might have since we really didn't know exactly where we were, or how we'd make it back to the lodge, or to the chairlift without the "guidance of our capable driver!" Not exactly the dashing sleigh ride of those delightful Christmas songs.

Some of us counted our blessings that it hadn't been as disastrous as it could have been. Many of us prayed we would return to the lodge without further *adventures*.

Sure enough, when we started back up that steep incline again, the driver stopped suddenly mid-way, causing us to grip the sides of the sleigh to hold on. We would have preferred gripping his neck instead at that point. The driver hopped down from his cab, and came back to the edge of the sleigh while addressing us: "I've never had that happen before, but in case it should happen again, please keep your arms and legs inside the sleigh." (Duh!)

Believe me … his message did not comfort us … nor did it build our confidence for the return trip! However, we did finish finally that sleigh ride and welcomed the open chairlift ride back down the mountain.

Once again, we hustled into the lodge for much needed refreshment and warmth.

So much for our collective and romantic envisioning of what we had hoped would be our "traditional sleigh-ride."

It wasn't very long, after our disastrous escapade over snow and ice, when we heard the Lodge's announcement: "Due to icy conditions on the mountain top, until further notice, all sleigh rides will be confined to the base of the mountain and around the parking area!"

Our consensus was: *about time.* We also thought it might be more suitable terrain for that la-la-land driver to manage ... or perhaps he'd even been replaced.

***

It was years before I attempted skiing again; but finally did with the help of a dear friend and professional skier. He first of all took me shopping for the proper attire and gear, which included a skiing outfit designed for warmth, as well as suitable gloves and a wool hat. The gear included properly fitted skis based on your height, ski boots, and ski poles. Back when I was skiing, we had the lined, basic plastic boots, pretty much according to your shoe size. The plastic shell contributed to the weight and stiffness of the boot. Our boots had heavy-duty plastic buckles that clasped. What a difference from those rented skis and boots from the 1960s. Today the fitting of ski boots is even more customized. They have that basic thick plastic shell with adjustable liners, which add warmth and help in sizing properly. Today they also use Velcro to fasten securely, rather than the plastic buckles.

When we returned from our shopping expedition, I donned the snow suit, went outdoors to put on the boots and skis. With both on my feet and poles in my hands, I stepped onto what appeared to be a flat front lawn. I became a little apprehensive and afraid of falling. It seems that lawn became *not so flat;* it was more sloped and rolling than anyone might have imagined. My instructor chuckled and said, "The first thing you'll learn is how to fall so you won't injure yourself." With Bill's expert guidance, I didn't exactly fall, yet, I was not as confident as when I was without the skis.

My lessons with Bill began with just that – learning how to fall on his not-so-flat front lawn. He taught me in falling to tuck and roll into a ball. Of course, wearing the well-padded snow suit provided all the necessary coverage, which made it seem less scary.

Now let me tell you how my sister and I happened to meet Bill, who was in his early seventies at the time, while I was in my early fifties. Katie and I were on a stay-at-home vacation, but we didn't want to sit around and gain weight. We'd go for two or three mile walks daily to avoid that. One summer evening, as we started that routine, we walked down through the Quaker Hill Elementary School yard, which also has three Little League fields and two tennis courts.

As we were returning home, we noticed two older gentlemen who had been playing tennis; they were sitting on the bench, chatting. They were obviously serious players and in very good shape for their ages. One was shorter and wiry with a twinkle in his eye, while the other was a little stockier, taller and more reserved; both appeared pleasant and upstanding.

As we approached where they were sitting, the one we would come to know as Bill spoke up: "Say, ladies, by any chance do you play tennis? It's a lot less strenuous playing doubles than singles." If you're not familiar with tennis, 'doubles' means four of us playing as opposed to 'singles' with just two of us.

I responded, "I've played tennis before, but my sister Katie hasn't."

Bill promptly volunteered, "I'd be happy to teach you, Katie."

We all began chatting. We learned that Bill Kelley was officially known as William E. Kelley, Jr. We discovered he was a high-energy marine biologist and was instrumental in the creation of the Mystic Aquarium. The other gentleman, Roy Taylor, was also a scientist, retired from Pfizer, but less outgoing than Bill. We shared with them our professions: Katie being a registrar at St. Joseph College in Hartford; and my being a trust officer with Shawmut Bank in New London.

After a brief conversation in which we indicated we had tennis rackets at home, we made arrangements to get together with these gentlemen the next morning. Our rackets were old wooden ones our parents had owned. Bill took one look at our antiquated rackets and told us to go shopping for new, lighter-weight ones.

Before sending us shopping that morning, he gave Katie a lesson in the proper grip of the racket. In the meantime, he sent Roy and me on to play.

After acquiring our new rackets and proper tennis attire, including sneakers to go with our shorts and tee shirts, we met Bill and Roy again the next morning. Bill started training Katie, who was not the most athletically inclined individual, but a good sport about it. Under Bill's tutelage she went from struggling and uncoordinated to looking more at home on the court and able to play the game well. We ended up having a lot of fun playing tennis, not only with Bill and Roy, but with others that we met too.

Bill was a gentle, patient, and calm, but very enthusiastic person ... an excellent instructor: the kind of individual who researched and read up on all of the intricacies of a topic of interest. He became a pro in each of these areas – tennis, skiing, gem stones, wine, and telescopes just to name a few. One could actually write a book on this man's life and his contributions to society – a most fascinating individual! Bill was often referred to as a Renaissance Man. By definition a *Renaissance Man* is a cultured man of the Renaissance who was knowledgeable, educated, or proficient in a wide range of fields. Bill was all of that and much more.

This reference goes back to Renaissance, Italy where resident Leon Battista Alberti (1404-72) expressed the notion he had that "a man can do all things if he will." The ideal embodied the basic tenets of Renaissance humanism, which considered man the center of the ultimate universe, limitless in his capacities for development, and led to the notion that men should try to embrace all knowledge and develop their own capabilities to the fullest. Alberti brilliantly exemplified these attributes in being an accomplished architect, painter, classicist, poet, scientist, and mathematician.

(For the record, I'd like to point out, the same holds true for women: capable and well-rounded.)

Let me elaborate a little on our dear friend and true *Renaissance Man,* Bill, the forever scientist whose driving interest in gems and minerals, harbored within the earth's core, drove him on passionately. His insatiable curiosity about marine life took in all the mysteries of the oceans; and his life-long love-affair with astronomy and all of its celestial wonders took in the sky.

As I indicated, Bill was a marine biologist, who had written several technical papers. He served as the first director of the Cleveland, Ohio Aquarium from 1954-64. During that period, he was also Associate Director of the Cleveland Museum of Natural History where he secured funding for the Ralph Mueller Planetarium. In addition, his passion for understanding the essence of precious gems inspired his becoming a Fellow of the Gemological Association of Great Britain. This gave him the opportunity to work with the extensive gem collection at their museum.

Bill was also the developer of artificial sea water which became known as *Instant Ocean.* It is a synthetic sea salt and simulates natural seawater for thriving marine aquariums. It was developed through sophisticated biological and chemical testing. *This creation of his is still used today by public aquariums, university laboratories, and home aquariums.* Instant Ocean provides marine life -- including the seals, whales, fish, invertebrates -- in the aquariums with what they need to survive in captivity.

As our own Mystic Aquarium, a non-profit marine life facility, was being developed in 1974, Bill and his wife moved to our area where he became its founding president. Bill worked very closely with the non-profit board to make our new aquarium world-class. Prior to its creation, we had nothing similar to it in our area. As I recall, the nearest aquariums were in the big cities of Boston and New York.

Upon retiring, if one could call it that, Bill became President Emeritus for the Mystic Aquarium. He and his wife eventually moved from Quaker Hill to Salt Lake City, Utah, and a few years later settled in Cottonwood, Arizona, where he had the chance to expand on his love for telescopes. The near magic of these intricate instruments, making things so far away seem so close, was all just part of the wonders of science.

Bill was also Founder and President of Opals, Inc. which had mining interests in Virgin Valley, Nevada, 1968-72. He devised a system to keep the valuable soft precious opals from crazing and cracking. This mine produced the famed Royal Peacock Opal, worth a great fortune.

He was a member and past officer of the Mingus Gem and Mineral Society in Arizona. As a member, he identified gem stones at no charge as part of the annual March Mingus Gem and Mineral Show from 1995-2010.

During our rest periods in tennis, or over wine with him and his wife in several evening visits, we learned that Bill had owned a small wine shop in New London. We don't know if he had become a connoisseur of wine before buying a shop, or while he had owned it. I do recall visiting with him and his wife in Arizona; Bill was then in his late eighties, and he was still the wine connoisseur and scientist, mixing two different kinds of red wine, thereby producing a burgundy. He was so excited about this wine; he couldn't wait for us to taste it. He was like a little kid in his exuberance. He poured tastes for us and was anxious for us to sample. Of course, before we could taste it, we had to first sniff the wine, take a taste, while swishing it in our mouths, then finally swallowing it. It was so delicious! When I got home from that visit, I went out and bought a case of each of those two red wines – Merlot and Cabernet – all to the delight of visiting friends.

***

Bill's hobby of astronomy began about age ten, building his own telescope from salvaged parts. He read extensively on the subject; there were never enough books on the topic. He authored several articles on astronomy which appeared in Sky & Telescope Magazine, as well as other publications. He was a member of the Salt Lake Astronomical Society in Utah for many years, enjoying the meetings, as well as public and private star parties. He taught classes on telescope making. When he was *ninety*, he created the OmniScope, which could be used as either a telescope or a microscope, as well as for viewing between those ranges.

Bill lived his life to the fullest until his passing at age 93 in 2011. He definitely fit the mold established by Leonardo da Vinci (1452-1519), the recognized premier Renaissance Man who exemplified these extensive capabilities and whose gifts were manifested in the fields of art, science, music, invention, and writing.

***

This amazing Renaissance Man was actually teaching Katie to play tennis and me to ski. WOW, what an awesome, multi-talented individual. (Too bad he wasn't driving the sleigh.)

We now return to my learning how to ski. After practicing tucking and rolling, while falling on Bill's front lawn, he emphasized not putting your hands out to catch yourself, or you might end up breaking an arm. This reminds me of my sister's taking up cross-country skiing. She started by putting on her skis, with poles in hand … all of this on our not-so-flat front lawn. Unfortunately, she fell and broke her arm. Unlike me, she hadn't sought Bill's expert instructions.

***

Once Bill had taught me how to fall, we went up to Mount Tom in Holyoke, Massachusetts where he began teaching me how to actually ski. From my previous banking adventure to Gore Mountain, I already knew how to ascend the slope by side-stepping or as they call it – *herringboning*. It is a method of having your ski edges cutting into the snow while climbing the slope by taking short, parallel steps, and being certain that the ski tips are pointing out. This basic maneuver was used when a ski-lift, either in the form of a toe-rope or chairlift, was not available.

Bill explained the need to traverse the hill -- skiing from side to side on the slope rather than straight down the hill. With his skis on, standing behind me, arms around my waist with his hands snugly clasped, we glided together while zigzagging and sliding down the intermediate slope. As we approached the bottom, he showed me how to stop by slowing down and angling the tips of the skis together with the backs of them pointing outward. They call it "snow plowing." We made several runs together before he let me go on my own.

Wow! Skiing was thrilling and exhilarating – I was so ecstatic that I could actually do it! And I was thrilled to achieve the intermediate (blue) level of skiing.

In skiing there are different ratings for the intensity of the sport. Some are color coded with green for beginners, the inexperienced level; blue for the majority of skiers -- the intermediates; and black diamond for the most difficult trails at a resort. Some resorts have instituted the *double-black* diamond for those truly advanced, more dare-devil skiers.

I had my share of falls – some more scary than others. One time I encountered a lone tree that loomed up in front of me,

124

directly in my path. Initially I had the feeling of being out of control but didn't panic; fortunately, at the last moment I applied what Bill had taught me about falling. I tucked and rolled into a ball, and fell on purpose, thereby barely missing the tree. Thank God for all those drills on Bill's front lawn.

However, there are those times when one falls unexpectedly; a ski goes flying off, and you end up falling and landing on your rump! You sit there in the snow, feeling like an idiot, bewildered, uncoordinated, and definitely not very graceful. It's one of the most dangerous and scariest parts of skiing all by yourself.

I have thanked God numerous times for Bill's expert teaching. Because of that, I was always able to get myself up and continue on. Being a conservative, careful personality, which carried over into my skiing, l was able to keep my bones intact.

Just the same, I have had my share of broken bones, thanks to a couple of casual mishaps. I accidentally broke the fifth metatarsal bone in my left foot, requiring a walking cast. This particular mishap happened while scurrying to my car to dash off to a business-after-hours function. While wearing clogs, I managed to roll my foot into a crack in the parking area pavement -- thereby breaking the bone!

Another time I was again rushing ... of all things taking out the trash. I was simply rolling the awkward canister down the driveway hill to the base where it meets the road. Foolishly, I was hurrying, while wearing dress shoes, so I could be ready for work. Apparently, the shoe heel was worn down and hit the black-top driveway the wrong way. Down I went into a heap! Talk about being stunned. I sat there in the driveway with the canister on my lap, one leg under me while the other was stretched out in front. I knew I had either a bad sprain, *or it was broken.* My sister Katie had already left for work. I was at home alone.

I managed to pick myself up, but realized I should not be walking on that leg! What was I to do? Fortunately, it was my left leg and I was still able to drive since the car was an automatic shift. I hobbled back up the driveway and into the house, then called the doctor who told me to get crutches and an ace bandage before showing up in his Niantic office. Of course, that meant I had to wait for the pharmacy to open at 8:30 A.M. I then drove myself the five miles to the pharmacy to get the bandage and crutches. With minimal instruction on how to use crutches, about which I knew nothing, I then drove another ten miles from New London to Niantic to see this so-called doctor.

When the doctor looked at my ankle, his "wise words of wisdom" were: "There's a fifty-fifty chance it's either a bad sprain or it's broken. (Duh! Ya think?) You need to go to the emergency room at the hospital for X-Rays."

I was beyond frustration at that point, since that was my very own intelligent diagnosis while sitting in the damn driveway. *Why didn't he send me there in the first place?* They would have had crutches and a cast already for me before the ankle swelled as much. Wouldn't you agree?

Fuming, I had already struggled with the crutches going up the doctor's steep driveway to get into his office. However, standing there on crutches and in pain -- while facing a steep blacktop driveway -- which I needed to negotiate carefully to get back down, was downright scary. I recalled Bill Kelley's instructions (of course, if Bill had been with me, he'd have already read up on the use of crutches and provided detailed instructions for whatever I might encounter) for negotiating hills on skis, so I applied that guidance, now with crutches. I carefully and slowly zigzagged down that hill, praying that no other car would come flying in. It was treacherous, but after an arduous journey down the hill to the car, I got in with a sigh of relief, and drove back to New London to the hospital. There, the X-Ray showed that the bone was indeed fractured.

Of course, by that time at least a couple of hours had passed since the fall; the orthopedic doctor was finally able to put a hard cast on the swollen ankle. The cast was bulky and awkward. His instructions were "no weight-bearing." This made for an interesting drive home. You see, the cast took up much more room with added weight to the foot than the shoe I'd been wearing. Fortunately, my right foot was handling both the accelerator, as well as the brake, with no back up support from the left foot. But I made it home.

Fortunately, I had the presence of mind to call my friend Julie, explained what had happened, and asked her to meet me at our home. I knew no weight bearing on that leg and dealing with crutches was going to make entering the house problematic because of the three steps up to our front door. I remind you that I'd never had to use crutches prior to this mishap and especially so since no one had bothered to show me how to negotiate steps or stairs with crutches. God bless Julie, who guided me safely up those steps. I finally resorted to sitting on my rump and with both hands and the one good foot, lifted myself up step-by-step, finally entering and able to disengage the security system without setting it off.

Our home is one story, but at the time there was a slight drop down into my bedroom. You see, when I moved home, the back porch was converted to a bedroom. Of course, when you have the normal use of arms and legs, one doesn't anticipate normally such potential blundering. With Julie's teaching me how to negotiate steps properly using crutches, I was all set. Of course, if the bed had been nearer the door, I could have done a not so graceful belly flop down onto it. But Julie wasn't about to have me do such an undignified stunt like falling flat on my face and risking ending up with a bloody nose or, God forbid, even a broken arm.

Our dear friend Julie was a registered nurse with the Visiting Nursing Association of Southeastern Connecticut. She not only taught me how to negotiate steps with crutches; she then made arrangements for me to use a walker that was designed to do single steps – not a flight of stairs mind you – but in a way that would accommodate my entering and exiting our home. This particular walker had extended arms so I could lift my weight with both hands on it to maneuver my way up the steps, using my good foot.

That is, all the good one foot can possibly do in such a situation. Her instructions came in handy at that time. I'll always remember a familiar mantra: "Up with the good foot, down with the bad."

Obviously, these interruptions to normal life routines can make simple tasks seem like pain-staking ordeals. Try attempting to take a shower without getting the cast wet; or substituting a sponge bath for that welcome shower. Of course, there is always the uncomfortable soreness under the arms from using crutches. I recall having to call my dear neighbor, Tristan, one day when Katie was at work. I needed to go for physical therapy and to deal with the two front doors. One opens into the living room, while the other one opens out onto the porch. Forget about attempting to set the security system on the way out.

What's the solution? One should have a wonderful neighbor to call in such circumstances, like Tristan!

God bless Julie! With her assistance, I realized that once again angels do exist. I know so many people who have experienced various traumas such as those our military men and women have had to in combat. The horrors of amputations and having to learn to use prosthetics. It used to be these horrible situations arose from defending our country in wars. But unfortunately, today people are also being killed or maimed by senseless shootings or bombings in malls, theaters, schools, churches, and arenas. No doubt those survivors would agree with me on nurses in general being *Angels of Mercy.*

Speaking of nurses, I recall a 91-year-old new client who was a retired registered nurse. My assistant and I met with her at her bank safe deposit box to give her a receipt for the assets she was turning over to the bank for management. In doing so, I noticed that many of her stock certificates had her listed as *Mrs.,* while others had her as *Miss.* I asked, "Which are we to use?"

We found her response amusing, especially the way she said it: "My dear, let me tell you. I've been married, got rid of him. I like using the "Miss" because I like having people think I've missed something. Let me tell you … I haven't missed a thing!"

I think not only of nurses but also of our military... past and present, especially our special recognition of them on Veterans Day. I also think of our glorious Statue of Liberty and how meaningful it is in welcoming immigrants into our beautiful country and welcoming our military home. I know when I see it as we approach JFK Airport in New York, my eyes still fill with tears.

In 1949, a musical, *Miss Liberty*, opened on Broadway. The inspiration for it from a book by Robert E. Sherwood. Irving Berlin wrote the music and the lyrics. Robert Sherwood was deeply moved when he saw what the Statue of Liberty meant to American GIs who were shipped overseas. He wanted to write a story about this symbol of freedom. He actually had crossed the Atlantic on the Queen Mary with fifteen thousand recruits. He had been deeply moved and greatly impressed by the emotion the sight of that statue generated among those soldiers.

Within that significant musical was a song, including the famous quote from the base of the Statue of Liberty: *Give Me Your*

Tired, Your Poor, which was taken from the poem: *The New Colossus* by Emma Lazarus. (Shared earlier on page 44.)

(Shared earlier on page 44.)

***

My incentive for learning to ski at that time was a slender, good looking man I was dating, who had just learned how the previous year. My thought was, I wasn't really that far behind; I could just take some lessons and join him.

Once I had learned to ski from Bill, this male friend and I would often drive up to Mount Tom and ski in the evening. We then decided to make a weekend of skiing and booked an inn at Mount Snow, Vermont. I thought it would be something we could do together. But even though Bill had trained me on the intermediate level, I wasn't at all familiar with the various trails at Mt. Snow. Burt had his own ideas, along with a brimming confidence in his skills. He was anxious to get to the slopes; so off he went, leaving me to fend for myself.

What amazed me during that skiing adventure was that I thought my friend and I would be sharing at least a single ski run or two together. Just like when he took me ice skating, I anticipated skating with him, but no he'd be off on either the slopes or skating on his own, leaving me all on my own. Until I built up my confidence by skiing and skating, I found it nerve-wracking and scary being on my own. *It was all so new to me.* However, he was gracious enough to accompany me for dinner at the lodge. (That was really big of him, don't you think?}

Since I was free during the day, that was when I would go skiing. So, map in hand I would trek the various trails, taking advantage of the color-coded directions that informed me of which paths to take. The various skill levels were clearly marked: beginners, intermediates, and adventurous black diamond. Once there, and actually beholding those slopes, they appeared a lot steeper than even the intermediate level at Mt. Tom. Hence, I decided to warm up on the beginners' slope. But even that one was pretty scary. So, I decided to take another lesson. With that lesson and a few runs, I felt much more in control. I had regained my confidence. I then moved on to the intermediate level and enjoyed a morning of skiing all by myself. Of course, by then my charming boyfriend was nowhere in sight. No doubt he'd moved on to the more expert and dangerous black-diamond terrain and couldn't be bothered with a mere novice like me.

Let me tell you some more about this … boyfriend. He was a businessman working for the government. He obviously liked being in control and alone where he could really shine. The guy must have been insecure; God forbid that anyone should outshine him, least of all a woman.

For example, he fancied himself the expert on recumbent bikes. The biggest difference between the recumbent and the traditional bike is the rider is in a more comfortable and natural body position on the recumbent, which helps reduce body fatigue and eliminates muscle soreness in the upper body. The seat is more comfortable usually with a back. If you have worked out in a gym and have tried the different bicycles there, you may very well have tried this one. It truly is much more comfortable, especially with older people or those who suffer lower back problems.

As Burt described the recumbent bike to me, telling me how you must *recline* while peddling, my literal mind pictured him somehow lying back on the bicycle and peddling, which to me did not sound at all comfortable. Of course, we didn't have cell phones at that time to search the internet for details. He had made it clear that we would not be biking together; he liked the tranquility of venturing alone where and when he wanted to go.

Remember how I mentioned a male friend calling me two days ahead of a bank-sponsored, annual black-tie event and telling me I was *too public a figure?* Well, that was Burt. As I think back, while we were in line for chairlift tickets, there were two people ahead of us who knew me from our home area. It didn't surprise me that we would run into people we knew, but it shook Burt apparently. With Mt. Snow being about a three-hour drive from New London, Connecticut, and a lot of people making the trip to ski, you're bound to run into somebody you know. That seemed to be more than Burt could handle.

The next year, it was interesting to me, while attending that same annual black-tie event, whom did I see? Burt there with a date. I was first of all surprised to even see him at the event, but even more so when he and his date sashayed up to the dance floor and he began twirling her around. They appeared almost to be professional dancers. It wouldn't surprise me if his date was his dance instructor. I never saw him or his date again at one of these events or any of the others; I suspect they had attended just for show, and they indeed had made a spectacle of themselves.

Skiing was great fun. I loved doing it at Mount Snow, where it was so peaceful and serene, as well as beautiful. After happily breaking up with Burt, I would often go there for a day or a weekend, which was absolutely delightful, especially spring skiing. That was until our friends, ski instructor Bill and his wife, moved to Salt Lake City, Utah. They invited my sister and me to visit. Bill took me skiing at Alta and Park City Resorts. Now, those were

magnificent and gorgeous skiing slopes with their fresh powder …
and absolutely *no dangerous ice.*

However, with the approaching spring warmth, not only did
the snow melt; but it also loosened rocks which rolled down the
mountainside onto the only paved, two-lane access road. After
enjoying a day of skiing, we were returning to our friends' home,
when one such rock roared down the mountain, catching the splash
pan under my rental car. The car stopped dead in the middle of our
travel lane – all of its oil spilling out.

There were a lot of people traveling the road that busy
afternoon … some who offered *no help* but *yelled* at us to "get out
of the road!*"* (As if we could have moved in the first place). A
very pleasant and friendly police officer happened along, stopping
to see if we were okay, and assessed our situation. This was
obviously a common occurrence for the natives; but not for us. The
officer told us how he made frequent trips up and down the
mountain and said: "I'll keep checking on you each trip to be sure
you're okay."

That was most reassuring.

There was one very friendly, wholesome, gracious family who stopped and offered us assistance. They assessed our plight and out of the goodness of their hearts offered to drive my sister Katie down to the mountain base where she could use a pay phone to call (no cell phones back then) the car rental company, who in turn would send a replacement vehicle for us.

We were a little hesitant to accept their welcomed offer since we knew nothing about this family; but what were we to do. We didn't have any idea how far a walk it would be to the base, nor what we'd find; then there was always the climb back up that treacherous, busy, steep mountainous road. We figured they would leave Katie at the store; I'd have to find her once I was mobile again. They appeared to be very caring and, sincere. They had a spiritual air about them ... Mormons perhaps. We accepted their most kind offer and they became our Good Samaritans, even to driving my sister back up the mountain to join me for our wait. God bless those angels ... obviously heaven sent!

140

All we could do was sit there in the travel lane and wait. This unfortunate episode was well before cell phones became popular and eliminated pay phone booths, pretty much entirely.

Chapter 7

Community Service

In remembering the period that stretched between the mid-
1960s and the-mid-1990s, the job description of bank officers, with

Hartford National Bank and its successors, Connecticut National

and Shawmut, included twenty percent of one's time being spent in

the community. Naturally you had to make sure your bank work

was done but you had the freedom to take time from your bank

schedule to volunteer for charitable non-profit organizations. In

fact, they would often recommend non-profit agencies with whom

we could work.

One of our officers who moved out of the area had been

treasurer for several years of the Family Services of Southern New

London County, a social services entity. It was recommended that I

take his position as treasurer. Up until then, I'd only managed my

own checkbook; but I loved working with numbers, so I said,

"Yes!"

That for me was a valuable learning experience. The board was comprised mostly of social workers or psychiatrists. They were determined to do right by our clients, fulfilling our mission … no matter the cost. But I was a banker, responsible for the agency's funds. I took my position seriously, and would ask: "How are we going to pay for this newly needed program?"

Obviously, I was new to the board, not having served on any other boards previously, and learning the workings of charitable non-profit boards and such agencies. It appeared to me that they didn't want to face the reality of funding. They would generally give me a well-rehearsed, pat answer: "Oh, money will come in."

With my faith, I believed the Lord would provide. But … we still needed reserves in case of emergencies or government shutdowns. I was raised to save for that proverbial *rainy day* and one did not dare go into one's sacred savings. I had always heard my aunts and parents talk about the 1929 Great Depression, the infamous stock market crash; the hardships people had to endure back then and how that devastated so many of them. People lost

143

their jobs; they panicked, and many felt desperate in not knowing what to do. Some folks broke up furniture from their homes to burn in order to provide heat; others committed suicide because they felt helpless and unable to provide for their families.

***

When you're dealing with volunteers in non-profits, even though the natural flow of moving up the ladder from secretary or treasurer to the board, vice president is usually the next rung before becoming president; or possibly a president-elect position in between. You can imagine my surprise when, after serving as treasurer for three years, the nominating committee, in its infinite wisdom, asked me to assume the presidency. I can only think that while they didn't seem to appreciate my questions, they must have decided I actually had a good head on my shoulders.

I really learned what it was like working for non-profits and awaiting receipt of state or federal funds, along with grants, and donations. My understanding is that non-profits continue today with these same financial challenges.

Some non-profit agencies have established investment accounts in the form of *endowments,* which help the agency especially in lien times, which occur from economic recessions, stock market setbacks, and hopefully not another deep depression with yet another stock market crash.

There are basically two types of endowments. The first one being *permanent* in which the principal, capital, or savings *cannot be touched for any reason* and from which only the income (dividends and interest) and possibly the appreciation from the stocks can be used.

The second type is *quasi-endowment,* whereby the agency sets aside reserves temporarily for special projects such as a roof repair or replacement, or a future building addition for expansion, or a special program such as community outreach dealing with behavioral health issues, medical, dental, school-based health centers, or eldercare.

Once I became president, it was then that our long-time executive director decided to leave the area for another position out-of-state. We hired his replacement. In addition to the stress of dealing with a new executive director, (as mentioned previously), mom was taken ill in 1978. We came so close to losing her, which brought more stress into our lives. That particular presidency became an education unto itself. Without getting into the confidential human resource issues at that time, we got through it, and the agency continued serving its clients.

Following that presidency, I went on to serve as president of a number of other non-profits including: Big Brothers/Big Sisters of Southeastern Connecticut. This charitable organization matched fatherless boys with men who would become advocates for them. The men volunteered their time working with the boys, sharing in sports events, and developing a strong male relationship while becoming a role model for youth.

The same was true for girls without moms. Women would volunteer and become big sisters to these girls, many times helping them through their difficult teen years.

I learned a lot from these two special non-profit organizations, which also gave me insights into the *for-profit* male-dominated business world. An interesting side note, non-profits generally *do not* pay wages as high as for-profit institutions. Consequently, we saw women as executive directors of non-profits, long before being elevated to higher positions in the male-dominated business world.

***

Coming up through the ranks in banking was an enlightening experience. First of all, as a new secretary, the other ones would deliberately tell you the wrong way to do something, expecting you would get in trouble for it. If you were late coming back from lunch, the other secretaries would tell on you. Of course, 'The Boss' told me to take a little longer lunch one particular day and I had his permission to take a longer lunch in order to celebrate the holidays with a friend. You should have seen the stunned looks on their faces with that tidbit of information.

Those other employees were not known for putting in extra time. However, the one from whom I learned the most -- who became a good friend and confidant -- and I were not afraid of putting in extra time, as needed.

When the only woman trust officer in our department died suddenly from breast cancer in 1969, I was promoted to her position. Leaving my secretarial duties behind, while assuming new responsibilities in moving up in the same department, was also challenging; *especially when her secretary became mine.* I was beginning to learn life's lessons the hard way – first-hand on-the-job experience, or as the old adage goes: *The School of Hard Knocks.*

Meanwhile, there was a young man, a Cornell graduate, who was also working in our department and moving his way up. He didn't think much of having to compete with a young woman who didn't even have a bachelor's degree, since he was so impressed with his "Cornell Degree." It did not matter to him that we were both promoted at the same time to administrative assistants and, subsequently, to trust officers a few years later. (And me without an Ivy League degree.)

In fact, after a particularly long hard winter, there was one really nice, balmy spring day when I happened to make the comment: "It's a nice day to get out and make customer calls."

His immediate response: "You stay in the office. Brad and I will go out on calls. You're low *man* on the Totem Pole!" With that comment, my question to myself was: "Since when?" I'd been thinking, for some time, that in our office, the "tail was wagging the dog."

He eventually left our bank for a *better position* with another bank. Personally, I was glad to see him move on and become an itch in someone else's side.

When I saw the documentary on Justice Ruth Bader Ginsburg, first woman ever appointed to the United States Supreme Court -- *a must see* -- she talked about being in the first law class to admit women at Harvard University. She then mentioned how her husband and she had had to move to New York City, her spouse having accepted a job there. This move for her meant she had to transfer from Harvard Law to another Ivy League college, Cornell to complete her law degree. In the documentary, she talked about the male culture at that time at both universities and how anti-women they were. In hearing what she went through, my mind flashed back immediately to the *Cornell male graduate* with whom I'd had to deal in the early to mid-1970s.

In hindsight, that young man did me a huge favor by getting my Irish up. I looked into college degree programs at University of Connecticut and University of Rhode Island. However, between the traveling distance and the six-month campus residency requirements, I opted for a Coordinated-Off-Campus Degree Program at Upper Iowa University in Fayette, Iowa.

By that time, I had accumulated sufficient curriculum equivalent credits for the first two-years through the American Institute of Banking, plus Central Connecticut State College. Consequently, I had only two years of studies left to complete my Bachelor of Arts Degree in Business Administration. I was able to take the majority of the courses through independent study. I completed the necessary courses outside of the classroom, on my own time. I would receive the textbooks and the assignments which I needed to complete. A faculty advisor was always just a long-distance phone call away. Of course, my exams had to be supervised by either an attorney or a notary to assure the university that I wasn't cheating. I was seriously earning my academic credits.

Today we have online courses available, so one can work full-time and yet complete studies for a formal degree. In this day and age, the big advantage to the student is it's affordable without the outlandish student loans upon graduation.

Upper Iowa University's residency requirement at that time was six credits in three weeks. I knew if I took that three-week vacation, I could meet those requirements without jeopardizing what I'd already achieved while on the job. And I could do all this within the Southeastern Connecticut community. I opted to go to Iowa in January for the three weeks. At that time, I wasn't into skiing or any other outdoor winter sports. I knew I would be indoors either all or most of the time. Of course, I had never experienced the mid-west cold temperatures, but I surely did during those *chilling three weeks.*

In fact, the first week we were on campus, the dean coordinated rides for all of us Catholics to go to Mass on Sunday. The second week, there was no such offer. My knowing where the church was, roughly a mile from campus, I decided to walk there. The temperature was dreadfully well below zero. I walked briskly for that fifteen to twenty-minute trek. By the time I had reached the church, my face hurt, my nose was numb – so were my cheeks -- and the tips of my ears were red from the cold. Mind you, they were well beyond rosy. I could barely feel my toes in the boots. It fell just shy of my developing frostbite.

That bitter cold adventure reminded me of author Jack London's classic short story: *To Build a Fire.* His tale was of a man hiking alone with his dog in *seventy-five below zero* weather over the rough snow-covered Yukon terrain … no plowed trail for them. Fortunately, my own adventure was walking on a plowed sidewalk and road over hilly terrain, similar to our village of Quaker Hill … one cannot get out of our village without going up a steep hill. It was a bright sunny day; but the sun, while a cheerful orb, was definitely not providing any heat. Remember that disastrous sleigh ride at twenty below zero I suffered? The beauty of the twinkling snow-covered ground glistened through the trees as I made my way to church. *I was determined to make it;* no turning back for me. I knew there would be warmth in that church.

At that point I learned how caring and friendly Iowans truly are. A couple, having seen me walking to church, made a point of asking me if I was a student at the university, and if I'd like a ride back to the campus. They also cautioned me that I should not be walking in such extreme cold. Mind you, freezing is thirty-two degrees Fahrenheit; this was well below zero and my introduction to *bone-chilling cold.*

I was most grateful for their guidance and the ride back to campus following Mass. (Another enlightening lesson I had learned.)

Usually, the dorm was hot ... and I mean *HOT*. At one point, we lost heat. It was bitter cold in that dorm. Not as cold as outside, mind you; because by then it was the equivalent of sixty below zero. Yes, I said *sixty below zero*. What do we know about dressing for the cold here in Connecticut? But in Iowa, as in Oklahoma, where winds come whipping down the plains, ... BBBrrrrrrrr! I shiver just thinking about it.

It turned out those six credits were the toughest I ever had to earn. I was taking three credits each in economics and in music appreciation. I really had thought the economics would be the more difficult because I had had a lot of musical training over the years – or so I thought. However, that music appreciation course was by far the most difficult. I came home realizing how little I really knew about music in spite of having had lessons in piano, violin, voice, and later in life, classical guitar. In fact, it took me quite a while before regaining that love for music, thanks to my sister Katie.

With her working at the Hartt College of Music, a division of the University of Hartford, where we enjoyed concerts and operas, I gradually gained a real appreciation for the music and theater as well. In fact, Katie created two paintings that were used as part of the scenery for the opera, *Aida,* by Giuseppe Verdi. The libretto was written by Antonio Ghislanzoni and was set in the Old Kingdom of Egypt. The opera was commissioned by Cairo Khedivial Opera House and the premiere was there on December 24, 1871. Katie was part of the chorus that sang in Hartt College's production of that memorable opera.

Even though we were only on campus for three weeks, we really earned those six credits. I can assure you that neither one of these was a gut course. They were complete with term papers and tons of homework. I was so grateful I knew shorthand. I took all of my class notes that way, and in the evening would transcribe them, thereby allowing the contents to sink into my brain. For the music appreciation course, we had to attend concerts and analyze the music. And by the time I had distanced myself from the actual course, and was back at home, I finally developed a true appreciation for classical music.

While working on and completing my Bachelor's Degree in 1975, my boss, along with several of the middle-management men in the bank, belonged to The Thames Club. It was an exclusive male social club, established in 1869 ... now over 150 years old. It is located in the historic district on the corner of State and Washington Streets in downtown New London, which was conveniently just across Washington Street from our bank's trust department. Most of the business and professional men in New London, especially those in management, belonged to "The Club."

Of course, at that time, there were also the Rotary, Kiwanis, and Lions clubs, which also were male-only members. Depending upon the community in which the club was situated, those service clubs provided members the choice of attending meetings either at breakfast, lunch, or dinner, Monday through Friday. For women, there were Soroptimist, Zonta, Altrusa clubs, and American Association of University Women. While the New London Rotary, Kiwanis, and Lions clubs usually met at noon during the week, the women's organizations met in the evening after work. By the end of the workday, most married women had to hurry home from work to take care of their husbands and children, and prepare dinner; in other words, *family time*. Consequently, the women's clubs were more for single, older women who had no family commitments.

The late 1960s to mid-1970s were known for all of the women's liberation movements: *marches, placards, and bra-*

burning. Gloria Steinham's name was constantly in the news, with not only speaking on women's issues, but also numerous articles on the topics. She has a fascinating biography, which includes founding the Women's Action Alliance, pioneering with national information in nonsexist, multiracial children's education. In addition, she was a pioneer with the National Political Caucus to advance the numbers of pro-equality women in elected and appointed offices, both at state and national levels.

The November, 2019 issue of *National Geographic* reflects on four hundred successful women, who made a major difference in the lives of women. There was a wonderful picture from the 1971 Smith College graduation, in which the Class of 1921, celebrating its fiftieth reunion, marched in its procession. One marching alumna carried proudly a placard that read: "We've come a long way, baby ... from Adam's Rib to Women's Lib."

It should be noted that in 1875, Smith College opened in Northampton, Massachusetts with a mere fourteen students. Today, Smith is among the largest, most prestigious of women's colleges in the United States, with students from forty-eight states and sixty-eight countries. It is an independent, nondenominational school. Smith is strongly committed to the education of women at the undergraduate level. They now admit both men and women as graduate students.

***

This was also the time when we began to hear of Attorney Ruth Bader Ginsberg, who was serving as the Director of the Women's Rights Project of the American Civil Liberties Union. She argued successfully, on their behalf, six landmark cases on gender equality before the U. S. Supreme Court. In 1980 this remarkable woman was appointed by President Jimmy Carter to the U. S. Court of Appeals for the District of Columbia. In 1993 she was appointed by President Bill Clinton as the first woman justice to the U. S. Supreme Court. Her biography is also absolutely fascinating! I share with you a quote from her biography:

"As a judge, Ruth Ginsburg favors caution, moderation and restraint. She is considered part of the Supreme Court's moderate-liberal bloc presenting a strong voice in favor of gender equality, the rights of workers, and the separation of church and state."

These are just two examples of fabulous women role models at that time who encouraged us to follow our dreams and keep putting one foot in front of the other, while standing up for our shared equal rights.

It was during this period, my boss, upon returning from lunches at The Thames Club, would tease me about marching up and down State Street, New London in front of *The Club* with my *placard* to encourage them to admit women. While I really wasn't into the Women's Lib Movement and not about to do as he suggested, he teased me once too often. So, I let him have it!

"Brad, I don't want into 'The Club.' What I want is the same as the men … or better!"

He responded in kind. "Well! In that case, you'd better start your own *gals' club*."

"Now, that's a *good* idea." I retorted. "I think I'll do just that!" I punctuated it with a jab of my forefinger that came within inches of his bony chest.

He tried mustering a clever response, thought better of it, and retreated to the refuge of his desk. Not another word spoken on the matter.

***

There weren't very many women in business and professional positions in the mid-1970s. However, I contacted other female bankers, women attorneys, and women accountants suggesting that if the men could get together once a week for a Rotary meeting at lunch time, and be gone for about two hours, *we* could have a luncheon once a month for an hour and a half. This was 1974 and the beginning of the Southeastern Connecticut Women's Network, now known as SECT Women's Network. We started the organization at The Ship's Wheel, a restaurant in the old Crocker House Hotel that jutted out onto the former cobble-stoned

Captain's Walk in downtown New London. Our mission statement: "The purpose of the NETWORK shall be to provide its members with the opportunity to meet other professional and business people, to communicate and exchange general and career information, to promote personal visibility and a sense of community, and to develop a constituency for the purpose of examining and speaking out on issues of concern to the membership."

Yes, being the individual who founded this organization, I'm known affectionately as *Mom* to that Women's Network.

We started with three of us. From that point we were each charged with bringing another woman to the next luncheon. This was our mantra. When we reached forty women strong, we decided it was time to formalize the informality and thus, the Women's Network was officially established in 1976. I was elected its first president.

We later created a second Women's Network in the greater Norwich Area because we didn't feel that we could take the time from work to travel thirty minutes to and from New London for our monthly luncheon meetings.

With the eventual merging of the Women's Networks from Norwich and Southeastern Connecticut, ours created a scholarship fund. This fund was created to benefit women returning to college, after raising their families, to help with the cost of their education at one of three state colleges within the Eastern Connecticut Region: UCONN, Eastern Connecticut State University, and Three Rivers Community College.

Oh, yes, while we started the Women's Network as strictly a women's organization, we eventually opened our membership and welcomed men into it. We did not have to change our bylaws nor our mission. Men wanted in because of the multi-business contacts.

Our mission remained unchanged.

163

**

At the same time the Women's Network was getting started, we had multi-talented business and professional women working together to form the Women's Center of Southeastern Connecticut: a non-profit to address issues dealing with rape crisis and domestic violence of which most of us, at that time, were ignorant. No one talked about such horrors. It was definitely before sexual harassment was discussed publicly.

There were eight business and professional women with Barbara Greenberg the leading force in developing the Women's Center. Talk about a wonder woman! She was a professional, working full-time at Electric Boat Division of General Dynamics in Groton. She became president of this new non-profit that had immediately established a *rape crisis hotline* manned by volunteers 24/7. It didn't take very long for the volunteers to realize, not only did the agency have to help our sisters in rape crisis, but also in domestic violence. As the needs of the Women's Center developed, Barbara Greenberg left her job with Electric Boat and

164

became the non-profit's first executive director. This agency then established a confidential shelter where traumatized women would finally receive protection, counseling, meals, and guidance in dealing with the horrible, life-threatening experiences in their lives.

Back in the 1970s, if the police were called to a domestic violence situation, routinely they would blame the *wife for inciting the incident*. The police would not press charges and one could not even obtain a court restraining order. But things have changed. Since that time, police departments and social workers through the court system have created partnerships with the Women's Center and developed programs to assist battered victims.

As the Women's Center grew, so did the needs of their sheltered residents. It was strictly women and children in those early days. That too would change.

The Women's Network members decided to adopt the Women's Center as its pet project. Members would bring in items to our monthly luncheon meetings, which would all be taken to the

Center to help meet the needs of their clients in the Shelter. These women (often with children) arrived at the Center with only the clothes (and bruises) on their backs. They had many needs, so the network members would bring in various sizes of slightly used clothing, shoes, travel size: shampoo, soap, deodorant, mouthwash, tooth brushes and tooth paste; the basics one would need for ordinary living. During the summer it would be fresh produce. One time, someone even brought in bananas, and a youngster exclaimed, *"What are those yellow things?"* He had never in his life seen a banana.

In 1984, Farrah Fawcett had the leading role in the heart-wrenching movie, *The Burning Bed.* That movie was based on a real-life story. Fawcett played the role of the abused mother of three young children who witnessed their father's numerous, vicious assaults on her. Accused of killing her husband, she relayed to the jury, blow by blow, what she had endured. She not only was acting in self-defense, but protecting her three children – she was acquitted.

Around 1991, the Women's Center also established transitional housing for individuals to eventually move from the shelter into apartments, so they might rebuild their lives.

The Women's Center of Southeastern Connecticut has worked tirelessly to explore the magnitude of domestic violence within our broad geographic area and what was precisely being done about it. Fortunately, most of us had never experienced first-hand the horrors of domestic abuse. We were naïve; but wanted to learn and help our sisters in need. It has become an invaluable resource for thousands of individuals -- women, children, and men too – hence the name changed to *Safe Futures, Inc.* Their mission is "… to save lives, restore hope, and change the future for those impacted by domestic violence, sexual assault, stalking, and sex trafficking in Southeastern Connecticut."

In 1962, when I was living in Boston and took an apartment with my roommate, we were in a five-story apartment building on Commonwealth Avenue. Our apartment was on the fifth floor. I share this while thinking back to that first apartment experience.

We didn't know our neighbors, although we would acknowledge each other upon passing in the hallway. However, during a lot of nights we'd be awakened by neighbors next door, obviously having a fight. To us it sounded like a drunken brawl. We didn't know the circumstances, but the screaming made us think the wife was being murdered! The pounding of what sounded like her head being smacked against the paper-thin wall, which was all that separated our apartments, was extremely scary to us, especially at two o'clock in the morning. We had no idea how solid or fragile those old walls were. Would they cave in at any moment, bringing the brawl into our own apartment?

My roommate from rural "Down-east Maine", and I from the Connecticut countryside, were both about twenty years old at the time. Neither of us had ever experienced anything like this before! We didn't know what to do. We felt helpless. And we hesitated to call the police on our own neighbors. Fortunately, another neighbor had called them on numerous occasions, because these rows happened all too frequently.

As a result of these frightening domestic episodes and the startup of the Women's Center, I have been involved with Safe Futures since its origins in 1976 – now over forty-five years old. Its official mission harbors the hope that if you, or someone you know, is experiencing domestic violence, bullying, or any other such form of assault, there *is* confidential help available to you. Incredibly enough, tragic situations such as these were deemed to be "struggles inherent in lower-class families."

We have since learned nothing could be farther from the truth.

Such atrocities have absolutely nothing to do with wealth, or the lack of, Domestic Violence crosses all socio-economic lines.

*I feel compelled to add that I adopted the life motto of my mom and her three sisters: "Let me live in a house by the side of the road and be a friend to mankind." Consequently, you should know this is why the entire proceeds from my autobiography will benefit Safe Futures, Inc. of New London, Connecticut, as they continue in their mission in being of assistance to women, children, and men. As I write this book, Safe Futures has a dream to create a *Family Justice Center.* The intent is to bring together in one location *all* of the services required to be of assistance to one experiencing these horrors. In this way, that individual will not have to be further stressed by running around to all of the resources available, each time having to repeat all the trauma one has been experiencing.

No one should have to experience such devastating, life-threatening assaults*.

***

Highly regarded Attorney William Miner was president of New London Development Corporation, long before it got involved with Fort Trumbull. He approached me about chairing the Alternative Building Codes Committee, which was part of the American Institute of Architects' redevelopment research, known as the RUDAT Study, the abbreviation for the Rural/Urban Design

Assistance Team. The committee consisted of community leaders and architects. Our charge was to look at ways in which State Street and Bank Street, the primary downtown business center, where real estate owners could make their properties more accessible in their renovations. One major concern was giving each property at least two egresses or exits. Our study even proposed the possibility of two adjoining apartment buildings, giving access to their two structures by connecting center hallways. We completed our study and gave a detailed report not only to the NLDC, but also to the Development Director for the City of New London.

I continued being abreast of what the NLDC was doing and eventually was invited to become a member of the Board. The timing was shortly after Claire Gaudiani, then president of Connecticut College, had also become president of the NLDC.

The New London Development Corporation, now known as RCDA or Renaissance City Development Association, in conjunction with the City of New London, and State of Connecticut, has done a lot for New London. Just think, without

171

that partnership, we wouldn't have the spectacular Waterfront Park or the beautiful Fort Trumbull State Park, nor the restoration of the then smelly sewage plant. We also wouldn't have had the House New London partnership: a true collaboration of *nine* non-profit agencies working together to enhance the New London neighborhoods by acquiring derelict buildings from absentee landlords and rehabbing rundown homes. Included in the nine agencies were ECHO, also known as Eastern Connecticut Housing Opportunities, and HOPE, as well as Habitat for Humanities. This was financially made possible by the endorsements and funding from the Frank Loomis Palmer Fund and the Bodenwein Public Benevolent Foundation, providing a multi-year commitment for funds to purchase dilapidated houses from absentee landlords, rehab them, while providing potential first-time home buyers training in home ownership.

When folks generally think of the NLDC, they immediately think *eminent domain* and the U. S. Supreme Court case involving *all* of Fort Trumbull and not just the "Little Pink House." I felt very badly for the people whose homes were eventually seized by eminent domain. I know I'd be devastated if the town decided to take my home through such means. Such unfortunate situations are much more complex than what is usually presented.

I have a strong faith that this area will eventually recover from that debacle, and the Coast Guard Museum will indeed be built somewhere in the City of New London.

Hopefully Fort Trumbull will one day be redeveloped.

***

We have always been a musical family. We thoroughly enjoyed gathering -- following Thanksgiving and Christmas dinners -- around a unique antique pump-organ, with its eighty-eight piano keys, and all of us singing joyously. We loved harmonizing while singing all of the old hymns, popular songs, and Christmas Carols.

I treasure the memory from childhood, our family of eleven gathering around the festive Thanksgiving table and singing, while standing, the first two verses of an old hymn as the blessing:

We gather together to ask the Lord's blessing
He chastens and hastens His will to make known
The wicked oppressing now ceases from distressing
Sing praises to His name, He forgets not His own.

Beside us to guide us, our God with us joining
Ordaining, maintaining His Kingdom Divine
So, from the beginning the fight we were winning
Thou, Lord, were at our side, all glory be Thine.

We also had a delightful family friend – affectionately called Aunt Ethel -- who was extremely talented musically. She played by ear rather than reading the music. All you had to do was hum a few bars for her; immediately she started playing the piece with full accompaniment, including the necessary chords and all of the melodic flourishes to boot!

My sister went on to have a double major in piano and English through the University of Hartford, which was formed by bringing together several prominent private colleges including Hartt College of Music and Hillyer Arts School.

Mom was also very musical. She was known for her Kindergarten Rhythm Band. Often on Saturdays at six o'clock in the morning, she would be up, playing the piano and singing. What a beautiful way to be awakened. We all became early risers.

Mom was Baptist and sang in her church choir. Pop was Catholic and mom therefore had had to agree to raise us Catholic, which she did. However, we learned to be ecumenical from the very beginning. At that time the Catholic Church had Parish Lines, assigning families to specific churches. Unfortunately, the village of Quaker Hill was divided in half. The northern half of the village went to St. John, the Evangelist Church in Uncasville, and the southern half went to St. Mary, Star of the Sea Church in New London. (That was actually the church in which Pop had grown up.) I so wanted to sing in the church choir, but we *"outsiders"* weren't welcomed to do so in St. Mary's Choir. I was happy that we were going to St. Mary's for my dad's sake, but really wished we could go to St. John's where we'd be with fellow classmates instead of all those strangers, who did not seem welcoming.

When I went off to Boston, I was excited and thought *now I can join a church choir!* I approached the priest at St. Ignatius Church, on the campus of Boston College, and learned that they had a ... paid choir. He encouraged me to try out; but in my mind, I was a small-town, deflated, naive young lady, and couldn't possibly be *paid* for singing in church. So, I declined.

Consequently, I enjoyed their glorious instrumental and vocal music until I moved to Waltham from Boston to be closer to the new facility that Hubbs Engine Company had built in Woburn.

All of that changed in the mid-1970s when Our Lady of Perpetual Help Church -- formerly the Polish Catholic church on Huntington Street in New London -- moved to Quaker Hill. This move occurred at the time Interstate 95 was being widened, including the addition of the second bridge over the Thames River. In 1983, the pastor asked me to become a cantor (leader of song) for the 9:15 A.M. Sunday Mass. He stated he would hire an organist. I said "yes" and he hired a multi-talented one, Brent Caldwell. Brent and I had fun working together until our dear pastor, Father Leo Sutula, retired in 1996. He was a very charismatic priest! A few years ago, I rejoined Our Lady of Perpetual Help Church in Quaker Hill and immediately joined the choir.

In the interim, I did join community choral groups including the New London Chorale and Cappella Cantorum, which were wonderful experiences. I just loved singing with the chorus. We would do two concerts per year, which sometimes included Mozart's Requiem, Handel's Messiah, or opera choruses in a wide variety of foreign languages. I've always harbored a love for foreign languages and in high school took French for two years. Later while working at the bank, my sister and I went to Centro de la Communidad -- the Spanish Center in New London where we studied conversational Spanish.

Since reestablishing my love and passion for music after that three-week, intensive music appreciation course, I have so enjoyed the fabulous Eastern Connecticut Symphony Orchestra concerts, the Eastern Connecticut Chorus, operas, ballet, and musicals at the Garde Arts Center, Ivoryton Playhouse, and Goodspeed Opera House, as well as Broadway musicals in New York.

Speaking of the Garde Arts Center, I have valued immensely being a part of its first two phases of restoration and renaissance. It was in 1985 when a group of forward-thinking corporate and private individuals came together to create a non-profit performing arts organization and to save the historic Garde Theater. Steve Sigel, the manager, was hired in 1988 and became a dedicated pioneer on its behalf. The Garde was built in 1926 during the golden era of motion pictures and vaudeville theatre.

To put it in perspective, it's one year before Babe Ruth hit his historic sixty home runs... and three years before the great depression. In all that time, the Garde endured the dread hurricane of 1938, World War II, the Korean War, and Vietnam.

The funding came from a true combined partnership of public and private institutions such as the previously described foundations of Bodenwein Public Benevolent Foundation and Frank Loomis Palmer Fund, combining with significant corporate and individual contributions. The Garde is now nationally recognized for its unique architecture and extensive range of artistic programming.

Today the Garde Arts Center, with its restored exotic Moorish décor, typical of movie palaces in the 1920s, virtually created a far-off land of mystery, romance, and glamour, has become the home of the fabulous Eastern Connecticut Symphony Orchestra under the direction of Maestro, Toshiyuki Shimada.

We are so blessed to have the tireless team of Steve and Jeanne Sigel managing this absolute gem with its highly diverse bookings. God bless them, their board, and all they do for the communities of New London County.

In every non-profit where I've been involved, fund-raising was *always* an integral part of what we needed to do. It still is.

Chapter 8

My Passion for Foundations

In banking, not only did we have the American Institute of Banking, which provided continuing education -- as well as the Women's Committee that organized the social events -- but we also had the National Association of Bank Women serving *women who became officers in banking.* It later became Financial Women International. It, too, provided an ongoing education ... more the practical hands-on kind.

For example, these courses addressed issues women were still facing in a male-dominated banking world, especially as we were moving up on that *proverbial ladder.* I recall there were many different subjects that one of us would obtain, read over, digest, and teach the other women officers during workshops. These included: Non-Verbal Communications, better known as "Body Language": what hand and arm gestures mean, as well as crossing one's legs; Oral Presentations – speaking before groups and the use of microphones; Personal Communication – proper decorum, non-use of slang, etc. This all came before the use of e-mail: Effective Assertiveness – proper meeting etiquette, when to speak up and how to do so; Listening – focusing on what is being said, taking notes before speaking up; and Negotiation: The Art of Getting What You Want – politely, but firmly. These various topics were most helpful to us all. It was a wonderful practical education that was also shared with members of the Women's Network as well.

Apparently, between the National Association of Bank Women and the Women's Network, local senior bank management was getting concerned that, perhaps, *we women* were organizing to bring in a *union*. In fact, a local bank president invited yours truly for lunch at the Thames Club, a downtown New London social club located in one of the city's historic landmarks. For this private luncheon, we were ushered into the Presidents' Room. He asked all kinds of questions regarding the two organizations, which I answered candidly for him. I also attempted to reassure him that *we had no intentions of bringing in a union.* We were just trying to support one another. It was important that we learn from each other in order to be prepared to move up in the ranks.

As I was rising in the ranks at the bank, I was given the opportunity to attend the New England School of Banking at Williams College in Williamstown, Massachusetts. They had a two-year Trust & Estate Program from which I graduated. Since the bank had paid the tuition for several of us to attend these programs, we were each expected to write up our experiences which became a part of our personnel files. I recall writing a memo to the boss, indicating my gratitude for the opportunity, and how much I had gained from the program. I also shared with him how important it was for me to continue my trust education by going the next step. I needed to also attend the National Graduate Trust School. For trust professionals, that program *was the equivalent of a master's degree.*

Four years later, the boss received a call from the trust department's training director, asking him if I would like to go to the National Graduate Trust School. In approaching me, the boss told me he'd already informed the training director that I wouldn't be interested, but was directed to ask me anyhow. The training director had made it clear to him that *the decision was not his to make.* Consequently, when he did ask, I exclaimed "Yes!" He was stunned.

This specialized training program would be over the course of three years 1976-78: complete with orals on the thesis in order to graduate. As I said, it was the equivalent of a masters' degree in the trust business. The only other ways of gaining the knowledge in the trust business were on-the-job training, or attending law school.

I, of course, completed the oral examination on my thesis ... before an all-male panel. My orals were scheduled for the last possible appointment on the final day of the program. That was a particularly grueling experience, *but I passed.* Thank God!

***

In 1975 the Estate and Tax Planning Council of Eastern Connecticut was formed as a professional non-profit organization. Its membership is comprised of professional estate planning legal, trust, and investment advisors. Its mission: to educate its members and inform the community through an outreach program on recent changes in estate planning and estate tax law.

In the spring of 1981, I was elected the first woman president of that esteemed, non-profit organization.

***

In 1983, the manager of the Stamford trust department left the bank. Just before he left, Connecticut National Bank had just hired a wonderful lady named Kate Clark. She was from Delaware, and thought she was coming to work for the manager who had interviewed her. Upon arriving at her new job, she discovered promptly that he'd left the bank for employment elsewhere. Kate felt abandoned. Management asked me to go down to Stamford, approximately ninety miles from New London, to help train her on our trust systems. I also had to acquaint her with our policies and procedures. I was in Stamford full-time, approximately a month, and then two to three days per week for a couple of months afterward.

I was asked if I'd like to manage that office, but I declined, thanking them for the vote of confidence. I told them I was happy to help out, but I really wanted to return to New London. I'd go anywhere they needed me, as long as I could come back to the Whaling City.

By that time, I had been working in New London for approximately twenty years. I was deeply committed to the 'Whaling City' and southeastern Connecticut with many *irons in the fire* that I wanted excitedly to see fully developed. These irons impacted greatly the arts, non-profits, and the business community in which I was intimately involved. I also loved working with my clients and assisting in their financial guidance.

That delightful woman, Kate Clark, became the manager of the Stamford Trust Department. We developed a beautiful friendship. I was available to her as a resource for some time after I had returned full-time to New London.

The other folks in that department – Stamford being a suburb of New York City -- questioned who was this "Millie Devine-woman-vice-president from New London?" In their childish way, they considered New London a-hick-town … and, therefore, treated me as if I were a bumpkin … a know nothing. These petty infantile people lacked professionalism and were utterly demeaning to me. They even tried booting me back to New London. I dealt with it quietly and professionally, and with the full support of senior management. I was therefore able to accomplish the goals they had set out for me.

In fact, an administrative assistant, who was working her way up through the ranks, and I attended a corporate dinner. The affair was in Greenwich at a fancy French restaurant, Cinq en Cinq. It included executives from a business that sought bank's Investment

Division's involvement in their own mission. That brash assistant had the audacity and the gall to issue me a *directive* before we even arrived at the dinner: "Keep your mouth shut, so as not to embarrass the Bank!"

My jaw dropped, but I chalked it up to simply being another part of my ongoing education. (For the record, I did *not* keep my mouth shut. In fact, I had meaningful and interesting conversations with every male executive in attendance.)

Meanwhile, in New London, several community people and yours truly had come up with an idea to create the Pequot Community Foundation in 1983. Its purpose was to benefit southern New London County. Today that foundation serves not only all of New London County – which includes, in addition to the city of New London, the city of Norwich, towns of: Waterford, Groton, Stonington, Mystic, Gales Ferry, Ledyard, Preston, Colchester, Salem, Montville, Old Lyme, Lyme, and East Lyme -- but Windham and Tolland Counties, as well. It is now known as The Community Foundation of Eastern Connecticut.

The foundation issues grant awards to non-profit organizations recognized by the Internal Revenue Service as 501(C)(3) tax-exempt entities. Today their endowment is in excess of one-hundred-million dollars and benefits so many people through these non-profit agencies. What a treasure for our whole *eastern third* of the state!

***

In 1987 the Eastern Connecticut Regional Trust Manager in New London decided to leave the bank for another position in Florida. The bank proceeded with a national search, which was normal, and I became the acting head of the region. I submitted my resume for the position. The bank decided it needed to conduct, not only a national search, but it was also necessary for them to interview the Community to see if it was ready for *a woman* in that position. All of the managers up until that time, as well as other male bank officers, belonged to The Thames Club; a private social organization to which I, a woman, was not eligible to join.

It took the bank four-and-a-half months before reaching a decision. During that delay, I was totally frustrated because they had women trust managers already in other branches throughout the state and four years earlier had *offered me that very position* in Stamford. I had a difficult time trying to understand why the bank felt it had to interview the entire business community. (Was it just because I couldn't join that prestigious male club?)

Their decision was made after yours truly, holding down her own job, as well as the acting manager's job, withdrew her application. I recall telling the boss that "I was not going to jeopardize my good reputation, for which I had worked long and hard to attain, *simply because they were not able to come up with a decision.*" As one can imagine, while carrying both the former manager's position as well as my own, things were about to begin slipping through those proverbial cracks.

About two weeks after withdrawing my application, the bank offered me that esteemed position as Regional Manager of the

Trust Department for Eastern Connecticut ... which I happily accepted.

Unbeknownst to me, while the bank was interviewing the community, Rotarians, attorneys, accountants, and other primarily male business and professional leaders were speaking up on my behalf. When I learned of their overwhelming support, I was honored, extremely moved, and most grateful.

My new position did come with its share of challenges. One example included the fact that I had a client and his family, who were accustomed to having their quarterly investment meetings at The Thames Club, along with their attorneys. Obviously, they expected to continue that arrangement. Fortunately for me, the attorneys were also members of 'The Club' and arranged for me to attend those quarterly investment meetings.

I was given extremely explicit instructions from the woman club manager as to what I could and could not do. I was allowed to *enter through the front door, hang my coat in the Coat Room*, and *then proceed directly up the massive staircase to the second-floor conference room* which, lucky for me, was right next to the ladies' room. The club manager would come in, take our lunch orders, and later deliver the desired meals. In the meantime, we had our confidential business meeting in a conference room behind closed doors.

Those quarterly meetings went on, as stated, for *five years*, until The Thames Club decided at its annual meeting in 1992 to finally open its membership to women ... *123* years after its founding! First thing the next morning, after that major vote and the bank opened, one of their active members and past president, Elwood McMorrow, marched into my office and graciously invited me to become a member. I said "Yes!" and became the first proud paying woman member. The club membership had given their Club Manager, Elisabeth Kienle, the honor of being the first woman member.

Movie buffs will recall the 1988 movie: *Working Girl,* starring Melanie Griffith, scrapping her way to the top in spite of her manipulative boss played by Sigourney Weaver.

No, I wasn't the first woman president. Nor by choice have I become president over these many years since 1992. The first woman president was a very talented lady, Faye Fathauer, who owned and operated her own small business: Quality Printers in downtown New London.

I've so enjoyed my membership with a wide variety of fabulous dinners, lectures, ballroom dance lessons, social events -- including trips to Broadway shows in New York. Of course, I'd take advantage of being in the City and usually joined a dear friend who resides in Brooklyn, for at least lunch at Sardi's. Sardi's is my absolute favorite restaurant with the *best*, in my opinion, Tahitian Vanilla Bean Crème Brule. Yummy! It is the one place where I definitely save room for dessert! If I had my way, I'd always order dessert first. You know how the saying goes: "Life is short. Eat dessert first!"

***

It was in July, 1987 when the U.S. Supreme Court informed Rotary International that in the United States of America, they had to open membership to women. In August, I was approached about joining New London Rotary. At that time, it took quite a while for the all-volunteer membership process and I was informed mid-October that I was accepted.

Within Rotary International, at that time, there was a *mandatory attendance policy*. Since my sister and I were about to vacation in Bermuda, I did not want my first *meeting to be a make-up* out of the country. Thus, I asked to be inducted in November.

Our schedule was accommodated.

It should be noted that there were, at that time, a number of Rotarians with over fifty years of *perfect attendance*. In Rotary, one can always make up a missed meeting by attending another club and receiving a make-up card that is turned in to the home club secretary.

As a matter of fact, following the 1938 hurricane, when the community was recovering from that devasting storm, and without power, the New London Rotary held its weekly meeting in the Roof Garden of the then iconic Mohican Hotel on State Street in downtown New London. They were served sandwiches and salad.

In December, 1987 the Club hosted its annual holiday party and invited spouses. Before women were invited to join, the spouses were all women and referred to as '*Rotary Anns.*' Once we women were members as well, we referred to male spouses as '*Rotary Andys.*' As you can well imagine, the title for spouses was dropped quickly.

I had an interesting experience at that holiday party, it being the first-time women members were attending. One of the spouses of a long-time member of the club spotted my name badge, confirmed that I was a member, and immediately grabbed her husband's arm, whisking him away. Obviously, she was rather insecure. I definitely was not interested in her husband; nor anyone else's.

While I was among the first women to join New London Rotary in 1987, I was *not* the very first. However, I did get involved right away in bringing five Rotary Clubs (New London, Mystic, Groton-Ledyard, Niantic, and Waterford) together to raise money for the Rotary International Polio-Plus Project. That international project's goal was to stamp out Polio worldwide. Each club provided ten members to work on our committee. With the help of another member, Isabelle Singer, then Executive Director of the Eastern Connecticut Symphony Orchestra, we brought the famous violinist Itzhak Perlman to the Garde Arts Center for a sold out – at that time the theater seated over 1500 people -- standing-room-only performance in 1989!

Rotary International President Hugh Archer flew in from Chicago to join us for the pre-concert dinner and the Perlman Concert. On stage we presented President Archer with a generous blank check. At that point we didn't know the total net amount, but it was projected to be a *huge* sum. As it turned out, the event raised a net of $73,000; $43,000 went to Rotary International Polio-Plus Project and the remaining $30,000 went to our own Lawrence + Memorial Hospital.

It was so much fun working with the other clubs and getting to know so many different people from all walks of life. All were working together on a badly needed mutual project. I highly recommend it. It should be noted that thanks to the Bill and Melinda Gates Foundation offering Rotary International a matching-gift opportunity, we have *nearly stamped out Polio worldwide!* This international project has also worked in conjunction with the World Health Organization.

It wasn't long after the concert when I was approached about going through the chairs to become President of the New London Rotary Club. Yes, I became the first woman president, serving the fiscal year 1991-92, the club's 75th Anniversary. We had a fabulous formal, black-tie celebration that year in April, 1992, which was the anniversary of the Club's forming, even though it didn't receive its official charter until June, 1917.

That year was also the 75th Anniversary of the Rotary International Foundation. Of course, we had to celebrate that, as well, within our District 7980, which covers the southern half of the State of Connecticut. We held a big dinner at Ocean Beach's Port n' Starboard Restaurant in May, 1992. Many out-of-town members and guests, utilizing their private planes, took advantage of the offered Fly-In to the Groton-New London Airport.

In planning these very significant anniversaries, our committee thought it would be great fun to have a big parade in downtown New London. We developed a list of dignitaries to be invited to march with us and extended the invitations. We weren't getting an enthusiastic response to the idea of the parade; consequently, after inviting everyone, we had to cancel it. I placed a call to our federal politicians' office to let them know of the cancellation. The office offered to at least send a letter in recognition of the 75th anniversaries, which I thought was a great idea. I asked, if by chance, they could do *two* letters; one letter to the New London Rotary Club, and the other to the Rotary International Foundation. Both letters could be mailed care of me at my address.

The Club's 75th Anniversary passed in April without receiving a letter. However, the Monday preceding the District's Celebration of the Foundation's 75th Anniversary Dinner, that last Friday of May, *a letter arrived.* I eagerly opened it, read it three times, handed it to my sister to read, to see if she read it the same way I did. "Indeed!" she said "Oh, yes, he's congratulating *you* on *your 75th* birthday."

My sister and I had a good laugh about that. We didn't say a thing about it at the foundation dinner. It wasn't until I was stepping down as President of the New London Rotary Club -- giving my year's summary of events and accomplishments -- that I informed the club how during my presidency I had apparently "aged twenty-five years" ... and why. Since I was only fifty at that time – my announcement drew an uproarious laugh from the attendees.

I was a member of New London Rotary for approximately thirty years and thoroughly enjoyed it. Rotary is a great organization and does so much good locally, on the district level, as well as worldwide. I now have been awarded an honorary membership in that wonderful club.

I'll always treasure my fondest memories of volunteering with both the New London and Waterford Rotary clubs in preparing, serving dinner, and even cleaning up after, at the New London Meal Center twice a month. I, for one, felt blessed by the interaction with the soup kitchen's clients, as well as the camaraderie of working together with fellow Rotarians.

As you can see, I have been intimately involved in southeastern Connecticut, especially in New London and Waterford; at one time the two were actually a single community. In 1801 the Town of Waterford, with its approximately forty-four-

and-a-half square miles, became a separate municipality from New London. It was an eye-opener to me when I learned that over fifty percent of the approximately six-and-a-half square miles of property in New London is owned by non-profit organizations: the hospital, a number of colleges, and federal & municipal governmental entities. All provide important services for the entire New London County. *All are tax-exempt.*

***

When I became the Eastern Connecticut Regional Manager for our bank's trust department in 1987, I officially began managing a wide variety of trusts and private foundations. Included in those trusts were the Frank Loomis Palmer Fund and the Bodenwein Public Benevolent Foundation, as described in detail in Chapter Three. Another fund, the R. S. Gernon Trust, was patterned after the Palmer Fund, providing grants to non-profit organizations located in the City of Norwich.

It was great fun meeting with executive and development directors in guiding them as they sought funding from these generous foundations. I administered all three of them 1987-96. I was able to help grant writers to understand why foundations encourage collaboration among non-profits, especially those providing similar services; or those that would make a stronger application by partnering with one or more compatible entities.

Overseeing the foundations, I would often ask if someone had spoken with a certain agency. Often the answer was "No … they're too elitist!" I encouraged them to reach out to those so-called "elitists," get acquainted with them, and thus learn from them.

When I retired from Fleet Bank and was starting my own business, I volunteered on the board and, in particular, the Distributions Committee for the Southeastern Connecticut Community Foundation. I did so until my business really got going, at which time I resigned from the board and that particular committee. By then I was working with many of the non-profits, presenting proposals, and I knew there would be a conflict of interest.

However, I recall while serving on that foundation's grants committee, I was given an application to review from a non-profit, that was well out of our geographic area. The applicant had indicated that it was collaborating with an agency within our territory. I happened to be most familiar with that agency. When I called the development director from the out-of-town agency and asked why they hadn't included a letter or data on the one with whom they were collaborating, I was informed that the Board wasn't going to be meeting for a while. Consequently, this meant they couldn't get the backing needed to meet the deadline.

I indicated that I knew this board met every month, so it seemed unusual to me there would be such a delay. I was informed the applicant organization had only just learned of our foundation two-weeks prior to the deadline, and was insistent on meeting the application's due date.

When you have been involved in foundations for a long time and have read as many applications as I have over the many years, you get to know those who have done their homework, and those who have simply thrown an application together at the last minute.

A lot of foundations today allow an organization to apply once per calendar year, if that frequently. Most public and private foundations today do *not* want to be written into the budgets of non-profits. If they did, they'd run out of funding and would be unable to support any new and innovative ideas; such as, curbing domestic violence, funding for rehabbing houses for first-time homeowners, for programs serving youth-at-risk, or for creative arts programs.

I also recall one particular application to the Frank Loomis Palmer Fund from High Hopes Therapeutic Riding in Old Lyme, Connecticut. That requested grant would benefit inner-city New London elementary school children by taking them out to Old Lyme to interact with the horses. That agency could not bring fifteen horses necessary for the program into the city. All of those children had been traumatized, having experienced the horrors of losing siblings or parents being shot right in front of them, or being abused themselves. I think of the Farrah Fawcett movie, *The Burning Bed*, in which three children frequently witness their father's assaults on their mother.

The Distributions Committee and I struggled with that proposal because it was benefitting a limited number of students. In addition, part of the application included round-trip transportation for the children. The language of the Palmer Trust was very specific to "*agencies in or operating in* the City of New London." We finally approved the application and, as with all grants, we needed a report on the results from the grant's expenditure.

High Hopes invited me out to Old Lyme to see firsthand the program in action and to view a short video on its impact. By the time I saw that program live, plus the video, the tears were rolling down my cheeks. I knew then and there that more children could

205

benefit from this program. I promptly encouraged the agency to increase the number of children involved the following year.

Most foundations want their dollars to be stretched as far as possible; as we say in the business: "G*et the best bang for the buck.*"

I think of the Rotary International Foundation and how funds raised by grass-roots clubs in local communities, such as New London, along with the aforementioned Bill and Melinda Gates Matching-Gift Challenge and the World Health Organization have nearly stamped out Polio worldwide. What a partnership!

With the Palmer and Bodenwein Funds we were also able to initiate projects such as the restoration of the Garde Arts Center and the establishment of the Pequot Community Foundation, now known as the Community Foundation of Eastern Connecticut. In fact, when we celebrated the 50th Anniversary of Palmer and Bodenwein, the bank published a brochure which had all kinds of pictures and recognition for the non-profits and the changes they had been able to create with the funds granted from these two private foundations.

There is no end to what can be done with imagination, ideas, creativity, and available financial resources. That is why I absolutely love being involved in foundation work. It is the creative mind with brain-storming and planning that makes things happen. I have had the pleasure of working with a vast number of intellectual and creative minds, who harbor ideas for practical solutions to solving the problems of human needs. It is so stimulating, exciting, and satisfying to see the results.

In this field, one never knows how many lives have been impacted. Just think of the patrons attending events at the Garde Arts Center, and all of the youth who have been reached through their partnering with the local schools. Not only the Garde, but Safe Futures, the Public Library of New London, other libraries and nonprofits contribute too. Once again, I think of my mom's and her sisters favorite saying: *"Let me live in a house by the side of the road and be a friend to mankind."*

207

Over these past fifty plus years, whether administering the funds or serving in some capacity with nonprofits, my passion for foundation work was born, nurtured, and eventually matured. My heart and soul will forever be in the trust, foundation, and non-profit world. My commitment to this all-encompassing passion will continue throughout my lifetime and well beyond. One can always learn more through innovative ideas and through the passion of others.

***

In the fall of 1995, it was announced that Fleet Bank was acquiring Shawmut Bank and rather than being Regional Manager, my *title* was changed to "Team Leader." While I've always considered myself an *agent for change,* those changes came rapidly. The year 1996 was by far the worst period of my fifty plus years in the trust business.

In February, 1996 Fleet Bank, having acquired Shawmut Bank, centralized the foundations statewide; consequently, transferring those special foundations from New London to Hartford. It was gut-wrenching for me to give up administering those generous foundations. Of course, by transferring those foundations, the bank tripled my account load, and reduced the middle-management title to Team Leader, as well as my responsibilities.

I was struggling to adjust to all of these changes, feeling I'd reached the lowest point in my life. While I had always loved what I was doing, it was now extremely difficult to get out of bed in the morning just to go to work. That was bad enough ... but, it was getting worse!

In July, 1996 the Regional Manager for the southern half of Connecticut called me from New Haven and asked to meet with me over coffee. During that meeting, he forced me to make the decision to *retire* as of January 31, 1997. He offered no severance package, but retirement for life with medical benefits. My inner thoughts were: 'I guess after all these years the bank *does not* think I'm worth what they're paying me.'

I knew that retiring for me was an option; but I had not seriously thought about it.

As of that date, I would be eligible to retire, reaching "the magic eighty-five," which meant, age fifty-five with thirty years invested in the retirement plan. This was no time to even think about retiring. Oh, no. Over coffee in a public restaurant? But that louse wanted that decision made right then and there!

We did not spend any more than half-an-hour before he declared the decision had already been made. I was retiring.

When we returned to the bank facility, he immediately spoke with one of the officers who had been reporting to me, and informed her that I'd be retiring in January. Thus, *she* would become Team Leader.

Believe me, I felt the rug had been jerked out callously from under my feet! He was happy; I was devastated. I felt as if I'd been punched in the stomach. Had my working for the bank for approximately thirty-two years all been for naught?

With that decision, I had approximately six months to figure out and decide what to do with myself for the rest of my career. How could I take what I had learned and use it to further myself? I made a vow that I certainly would never even consider another big bank. I was only going to do what was *fun* here on. In my head, *I was too young to retire.*

When the boss dropped that bombshell on me, I recall telling him the bank was now making a "leap of faith" off the Gold Star Memorial Bridge into a viable option. I don't know where that thought came from. I certainly had not been thinking of suicide. Perhaps I'd stepped into the shoes of actor James Stewart in his role as a banker, George Bailey, in the classic 1946 movie: "It's a Wonderful Life." To this day I get teary-eyed when George decides he still wants to live. (If you haven't seen that movie, it usually airs on most stations during the Christmas season. I recommend it.) As I thought about my comment and that movie, that combination gave me a better understanding of why people do feel compelled to jump off the bridge during such highly stressful times.

The next day that ruthless boss telephoned me once again. This time he informed me that the bank would be throwing a retirement party "on my behalf" and, that my successor was to plan it! This news did *not* put me in a party mood.

"No thank you," I said curtly.

He insisted.

I finally said, "Yes, on one condition. Human Resources had to give me the financial details entailed in this decision. If they could not accomplish that before the party in December, then the bank would have a retirement party *without its guest of honor*."

Because of the merger between these big banks, Human Resources was in the process of consolidating the details from the various smaller bank acquisitions ... in what would become the new pension plan. *Hence, they were unable to tell me for several weeks what I would receive for pension and what the medical insurance coverage would be.* They were probably just concerned that I'd sue the bank and were trying to reassure me how, after all, it had been *my decision* and not the bank to force me out -- in spite of my position having already been filled.

That entire chain of events created a swathe of uncertainty for me ...

I refused to sell my soul to that bank. I worked out my employment until January 31, 1997, when I officially retired from Fleet Bank (successor to Hartford National Bank & Trust Company, Connecticut National Bank, and Shawmut Bank).

At that time, there were numerous mergers of relatively big banks gobbling up smaller ones; some not that much smaller. The acquiring entity's culture was entirely different from the one being absorbed. Consequently, they were laying off older, higher paid officers and staff, and replacing them with younger people ... all who accepted lower pay.

In other words, the acquiring institution was strictly bottom-line driven, and displaying no semblance of a heart.

Chapter 9

My Continuing Career Life

I spent much time thinking, soul searching, and praying on what to do next with my career. I knew I had to face the reality, take all of this negativity, and somehow turn it into a positive. They were not going to crush me. It was a moment of divine opportunity to transform, to heal, to grow, and to learn from these horrendous challenges.

Immediately the King James version of the Twenty-Third Psalm, which we had to memorize in public elementary school, came to mind, which is as follows:

"The Lord *is* my shepherd; I shall not want.
He maketh me to lie down in green pastures;
He leadeth me beside still waters.
He restoreth my soul;
He leadeth me in the paths of righteousness for his name's sake.
Yea, though I walk through the valley of the shadow of death,
I will fear no evil; for thou art with me;
Thy rod and Thy staff they comfort me.
Thou preparest a table before me in the presence of mine enemies;
Thou anointest my head with oil; my cup runneth over.

215

Surely goodness and mercy shall follow me all the days of my life; and I will dwell in the house of the Lord forever."

With all of the courage and strength I could muster -- along with a big smile on my face -- in December, 1996, I walked into that dreaded, bank-sponsored retirement party. A dear friend joined me. It was Tom Gullotta, who was then Executive Director of Child and Family Services. He knew I'd been struggling with what I was going to do with myself. Consequently, he took the opportunity of saying: "I know you have your name in at a non-profit to do development work. But have you ever thought of going into business for yourself and working with a number of non-profits? We could surely use the help."

Yes, I'd thought of going into business for myself, but had not thought of that particular possibility. It was as if a light bulb began radiating in my head ... My prayers were answered – I'd been given guidance for my next career steps. I recall in my remarks, at the end of that party, making a carefully worded statement: *"I might even go into business for myself."*

The trust department management was stunned when the number of reservations rose to over three hundred for that party. I'm sure they had thought just a handful of people would want to attend. Among the large number of guests at that special event were former clients, business and community leaders, representatives from all of the non-profits, family, and friends. Included were my sister and my dear friend Beryl Hobart who had driven down from Maine to be with us. It seems that she and my sister had been in cahoots in putting together a surprise for me.

A memorable highlight from that auspicious occasion was a wonderful classical guitarist hired to play throughout the evening; another was the presence of fellow Rotarians, Lew Buckley and Pamela Akins. They added their own very special music to the program. Captain Lewis J. Buckley, then United States Coast Guard Band Director (1975-2004), had taken the theme song from the hit show *Thoroughly Modern Millie* and substituted words, which were sung by Pamela Akins, owner of Akins Marketing & Design. The words are as follows:

217

"Waterford, U. I. U. Williams and Northwestern too,
Alma Maters of Millie Devine
And we know that ev'ry one of them is proud of her
'Cause just like them we've all of us been 'wowed' by her!
Everything she does is thoroughly modern,
(Look at her proclivities)
Everything she does puts her out in front
(Look at her activities)
First woman president of Rotary Club
With her the Thames Club at last stopped giving
gals the snub! ___
She's led ev'ry kind of organization.
Many times she founded them.
People can't believe the things that she's done.
Often she's astounded them.
The Women's Network, the Transportation Consortium.
These are groups that Millie's worked with
to make our future bright.
Big Foundations are the things she knows best ...
Palmer Fund and Bodenwein ...
Helping make our whole community strong.
That's what makes her so Devine!
She has a vision of what we can become
And now, we've got to keep up the work that she's begun.
She worked hard to make New London a good place ...
thriving and respectable.
Now she fin'ly has a chance to relax.
Everything's neglectable!
The work is over; it's time to sing Auld Lang Syne.
So, thanks for all you've done from all of us;
Millie, you're Devine!"

The next day at Rotary those two dear fellow Rotarians performed this masterpiece once again. Following their encore presentation, they presented the sheet music to me.

I was extremely touched and honored!

***

An article in tribute to me had also appeared on the Editorial Page of *The Day* that morning. You see, we do a lot of singing at Rotary, and I was scheduled as the song leader for that particular meeting. Given the article regarding my tributes in that morning's paper, the retirement party the night before, and the hollow feelings of not being wanted by the bank *"due to age,"* I started my remarks with a variation of Mark Twain's infamous quote: 'The report of my demise is premature.' Consequently, the *old* song I chose for all to sing was: *The Old Gray Mare, she ain't what she used to be ..."*

Everyone joined in singing with gusto!

***

Following that memorable party, when Katie, Beryl, and I had returned home, my sister said, "I didn't know that you'd decided to go into business for yourself."

Beryl agreed with her – for that was what they had heard – but I recall having chosen my words very carefully, and having said: "I *might* even go into business for myself."

The three of us began discussing the possibilities for what I'd be doing and the name of my business. After determining I would do planned-giving, estate planning, development, and grants advisement, we tossed around some ideas for appropriate business names. We came up with *Devine Planning*.

At that point all of the pieces for my next career started falling into place. It was truly serendipitous!

The next morning, I was off to New London to have coffee with a friend. One of his co-workers, who had been at the party, saw me and said he had just the space for my new business. We

220

promptly made an appointment to see that office. It was the Tower of Harris Place on State Street in downtown New London.

The space was unique and beautiful on the fifth floor of Harris Place and was literally *a tower*, with at least six steps required to get up into the office, and a small storage area at the foot of it. The office had a total of five huge windows; three of them faced south and overlooked the rooftops of New London toward Long Island Sound. The other two looked down State Street toward the historic railroad station; the Thames River flowed by the train station, while the unique Eugene O'Neill sculpture rested by on the pier.

For a good part of my banking career in New London, I had offices with no windows. When I saw this space, my spirits soared! I knew my creative ideas would soon flow, and the business would definitely be a success.

Who would have thought, that at age 55 – when experts were *encouraging* me to retire – that I would be embarking on a brand-new career.

I called my attorney and shared with him our thoughts on starting my own business, as well as the proposed two-year lease for the space, and asked his thoughts. With his guidance, I went to my dear friend, Jeanne Sigel, who owned Island Design, a highly regarded and multi-talented marketing firm in downtown New London. I told her what I was thinking, the name, and my mission. I asked for her opinion since she was the creative one on the business name. Once we discussed the details of what I planned to do, her immediate response was, "I wouldn't change a thing. It's perfect!"

She got to work and apparently within fifteen minutes had come up with the logo and layout for business cards and a letterhead.

I hadn't mentioned any particular color to her – hadn't even thought about that minute detail. When she showed me the samples, I was ecstatic to see she had used purple – not just purple, but my very favorite shade ... *magenta*. In addition, during the period of my forced retirement from Fleet Bank, all I could think of was the poem by Jenny Joseph: "When I'm an Old Woman, I Shall Wear Purple."

I asked her how she'd come up with the color. She said she had thought about what I'd be doing, which would be helping people plan wills, estates, trusts, and gifts of all kinds. "Purple projects an ethereal image," Jeannie said. I agreed. The color purple also has many other positive connotations, including the *power of purple* used by Safe Futures.

From that point on, I became really focused and wrote up my business plan. On February 1, 1997, I officially opened the doors to my new business office: DEVINE PLANNING.

My official retirement date from Fleet Bank was January 31, 1997. Yes, I chuckled along with everyone else ... *I was actually retired for only a single night.*

The next morning in my new glorious office, I immediately went to work sending out letters to prospective clients -- individuals and non-profit entities.

Reactions were priceless. Everyone who heard the name chuckled. After all, for years, people had been having fun with my last name and would say: "Devine is so Divine!" I knew from those reactions to the name and what I'd be doing, especially with the way in which all of the pieces fell into place, this had to be the Lord's Plan for my future. What could be better? I'd be helping people in the trust business, the very thing I had been doing for the past thirty-two years.

My business was growing. I was helping a large number of individuals and non-profits, whether an existing program or someone starting a new one. Of course, I always encouraged my individual clients to review our estate and gift ideas with their respective attorneys and accountants.

I was approached by a representative of Connecticut College to teach grant writing in their Continuing Education Division. I accepted and did so for three semesters per year – spring, summer and fall. I held that position for as long as their Continuing Education Division remained. When that Division closed, I found a new home for the Grant Writing Course with New London Adult and Continuing Education. That lasted several more years,

Since I had administered the Frank Loomis Palmer Fund, Bodenwein Public Benevolent Foundation, and R. S. Gernon Trust for approximately ten years, I approached teaching from the funder's viewpoint, rather than that of a grant writer. Believe it or not, *I had never written a grant proposal*; but I had read, reviewed, edited, and guided many non-profits over the years in finding the proper resources and completing the necessary proposals. To this day, I still have never written an actual grant proposal.

While teaching that very grant writing course at Connecticut College, I also developed and taught a separate course: Community Stewardship. Peter Block, author and speaker, had been my inspiration to create such a course. He had authored "The Empowered Manager" and "Stewardship." He introduced *for-profit* and *non-profit* to the concept of "Choosing Service Over Self-Interest." Having served on numerous non-profit-boards, I had observed that many upstanding business people appeared to leave their business sense outside the door once they entered the non-profit board room.

You will recall that for-profit entities usually have stockholders who invest in their corporation and who also receive dividends. On the other hand, non-profit charitable organizations plow their surplus back into the programs and the services provided in meeting their missions.

Non-profits need to be managed as if they were *for-profits*. Consequently, my course covered board responsibilities -- the fiduciary responsibility of board members, and managing the non-profit. We covered the following board responsibilities: determining the mission of the agency; while hiring the executive director to manage operations, and supporting that individual, which requires at least an annual one-on-one meeting between the board chair and the director to establish goals and assess performance. The board is also responsible for long-range strategic planning in conjunction with the executive director; and it must ensure adequate financial resources, along with proper training. The board is also responsible for introducing new members to the organization and informing them of their obligations. Requirements include: attendance, ensuring that the highest image of the agency is maintained, and that financial resources are available. In other words, the Board needs to govern more and manage less.

***

Let me tell you about my landlord, I'll refer to him as "Mr. Smoothie." He was all business and had a property manager with whom tenants would interact. Mr. Smoothie did the *heavy lifting* of the business. He signed leases and smirked at tenants, while his eyes were shifting in all directions. He was usually sickeningly sweet in his greetings, and was generally impressed with himself, putting on airs, while looking down his nose at you. He dressed as a professional business man, generally wearing either a suit and tie, or at least a sport jacket.

My office lease ran out in January, 1999. I worked with my attorney in its renewal for another two or three years. Unbeknownst to us, while we thought we were dealing in good faith, Mr. Smoothie apparently had other ideas for *my* office space. I learned this by running into another female tenant in the Ladies Room one day. When she saw me, she immediately told me how she and her co-workers were going to miss me. Mr. Smoothie had apparently already told her and her partners that I'd be moving within a year *and had offered them my space.*

You see, my office consisted not only of the area I was occupying, but it also had plenty of space above that room. All it would require to expand the space was for *me* to go to the expense

228

of installing *a spiral staircase* to the tower floor above. That would double the area from 354 square feet to 708 square feet!

Now, I had no employees and no plans for hiring any. I did *not* need additional space, nor the added expense of investing in a spiral staircase installation … which would ultimately benefit the landlord and no one else. (How often do we run into people who are concerned primarily with themselves, with absolutely no regard for others.) For the record, I did not need my rent to double either.

When my sister and I learned of this news, I shared the information with my attorney. He listened quietly, and we agreed that negotiating with this particular landlord would cease. My sister and I then started looking for small professional office space in downtown New London, and in Waterford too. Not finding anything suitable, we spoke with a fabulous contractor, Joe East, who had done beautiful and meticulous work for us in the past. We shared with him our ideas about adding on to our home. He loved all of it!

Joe took the original space, which started as a porch, then a bedroom, stripped it down, and tripled its size to 352 square feet. This new room became my gorgeous home office. It was built out to the back of our home with its own private entrance on the north side of the room, keeping home and business as separated as possible.

The room is twenty-eight feet long and twelve-and-a-half feet wide. At the end of the room, facing the eastern woods, it is bowed and entirely glassed in with eleven Anderson windows that crank open -- two of them face north, seven face the east, and the other two face south. With a round, glass-topped, mahogany based conference table in that setting, it was ideal for confidential and relaxing conversations. The chairs are traditional, hardwood Windsor-style ones with arms. They are all black and brown with gold trim, and all have a logo on the back frame identifying the non-profits represented. I was thrilled when Connecticut College and Mitchell College, in separate presentations, gave their chairs to me. Because of the view from my tower office of the Eugene

O'Neill statue, I also bought a chair from the O'Neill Theater Center. Since my first non-profit client was Norwich Free Academy, I purchased one of their chairs, and acquired one from my alma mater too: Upper Iowa University. Since I was doing so much work with non-profits, this was a beautiful way of recognizing them. Older clients especially appreciated the sturdiness of the arms built into the chairs.

Imagine the ever-changing view from those windows! As I mentioned, we gaze out from the office into the woods that surround our home: the wildlife keeps us entertained, whether it is deer emerging from the woods during the winter, seeking food in our backyard; or bands of wild turkeys gathering, also looking for food. Of course, we also have foxes, coyotes, fisher cats, and bobcats, as well as other indigenous animals too, commonly found in our area.

Our woods are mostly a variety of oak trees, but mixed in we have pines, birch trees, maple trees, and sassafras as well. The change of season provides a magnificent variety of scenery from that vantage point. The woods originally belonged to our family, but today are owned by the Waterford Land Trust, preserved as open space.

I moved into my new home office the beginning of 2000. I was absolutely thrilled with it! Joe East, our contractor, designed the office with its own supply closet, a long wooden counter to accommodate the computer, printer, and workspace. Under this counter are a pair of two-drawer file cabinets, separated by a knee hole to accommodate anyone sitting at the computer.

My sister made sure I had an appropriate wooden writing desk. It is simply beautiful with its inlaid multi-wood center design. All I need do is swivel my chair around to utilize this gorgeous desk and its single drawer.

When my business was located in downtown New London, parking was always a challenge ... unless you were willing to walk at least the length of a football field from the parking garage, or clients were lucky enough to get a parking place on either State

Street or Eugene O'Neill Drive. Having a business at home eliminated parking problems. Of course, having a business at home also meant, if it snowed, clients canceled appointments; so, all I had to do was march through our TV room and strut directly into my office. No more driving through snow. (Yea!)

I've mentioned before that my favorite color is purple, so you know I have purple carpeting, purple ceramic cups for coffee, with other touches of that color as well. Such examples are my amethyst-colored stuffed teddy bear ... my mascot. And, I have a purple stuffed moose -- a souvenir from my Alaskan trip. For the longest time, I actually used pens with purple ink to sign all of my letters.

Chapter10

Life Changes

The year 2000, the fabled Millennium, was off to a great start. All was well.

My sister Katie retired from her then part-time job in banking. She was getting back to her beloved art work, taking lessons again, and we were doing some traveling. We vacationed in Maine that summer and made a quick trip back there in early September to see our friends from Kent, England, who were visiting Charlie and Beryl in Maine, while on the way to Canada.

However, into every life some rain must fall. A couple weeks following that trip, it came in the form of a deluge!

It was approximately 3:40 P.M. on Monday afternoon, September 23, 2000. I was about to leave home for a four o'clock hospital board meeting in New London. Katie and I were discussing her plans for the evening. She was bringing in the house plants for the winter from their comfy outdoor summer vacation.

She was going to mow the front lawn, come in, clean up, have supper, and then go to a church meeting in Norwich.

Shortly after I left for my meeting, Katie had finished bringing in the plants, and was mowing the front lawn. It couldn't have been long after she'd started mowing, when a neighbor, while passing our home, had found the lawn mower in the road … then saw Katie lying on the lawn.

The neighbor, who was an emergency medical technician, stopped and tried to help. She tried calling the emergency number but her cell phone had no signal. By then, others were stopping and offering assistance.

Our road is an extremely busy one, especially at that late afternoon rush hour. (At that time, cell phones weren't reliable in our area due to all of the hills surrounding us.)

While the emergency technician was tending to Katie, another neighbor drove down the road to the first driveway and then up the quarter-mile-long dirt drive to our dear neighbors, the

Ostronics. Fortunately, Valerie worked from home with her children's daycare center. She was there and immediately called for help from her landline. The neighbor returned to Katie and awaited, along with the EMT, the arrival of the ambulance and police.

Trembling from this shocking news, Valerie tried frantically to call mutual friends to see if anyone had any idea where I might be. She made contact finally with one such friend, who had previously served on the hospital's board. He stopped, thought; then realizing her work schedule, told her: "No doubt you'll find her at the hospital."

As that call ended, he dialed up another mutual friend, Henry Savin. Between Valerie and Henry, they reached Lawrence + Memorial Hospital and got the message to the hospital president, who excused himself from the board meeting and stepped out into the hallway. In the meantime, having been assured they'd gotten the message to the hospital's president, Henry rushed there to be with me and to assist, which also included driving me home.

(There is absolutely no way I could have driven myself home that night!)

***

Meanwhile, the board meeting continued routinely with the chairman following the agenda. The next thing we knew, the president opened the boardroom door a crack and motioned for *me* to join him in the hallway. I had no idea why he would be calling me out of that meeting. Once in the hall, I was informed that Katie had died of a massive heart attack while mowing our front lawn. I was stunned ... the wind had been knocked totally out of my sails. While shaking like a leaf, they helped steady me as they then walked me down the long hall to see her. It took me a long time to get over seeing her just lying there ... lifeless.

I was devastated and felt so badly that I wasn't there to get help for her. She was tended by strangers who didn't know either of us. A few days after that horrific episode, the EMT, who had attended to her, saw me driving into our yard and followed me up the drive. Of course, I had no idea who this stranger was, which was scary to me; but she promptly introduced herself as Lori Reynolds. She apologized for startling me, and let me know that she lived about a mile up the road. She told me she was the emergency technician who had found Katie lying on the lawn. Lori offered me her sympathy and reassured me that Katie was *not alone* when she had taken her last gasp of breath.

Ironically, Katie went the same way Pop had gone … mowing our front lawn.

From that day on, I *never* mowed my own front lawn again.

Thanks to family, neighbors and friends, I had a lot of support, which I desperately needed. I was now the end of my family line.

***

Let me expand on what these three special friends, Henry Savin, Beryl Hobart, and Valerie Ostronic did for me:

As I indicated, Henry came to the hospital to assist me and drove me home. (I would be remiss if I did not add my thanks to Bill Stanley, Vice President of Communications and Development at Lawrence + Memorial Hospital, for driving my car home for me that unbelievable evening.)

Let me introduce, officially, my now *big brother,* Henry Savin. He is a large man: over six feet tall with broad shoulders, and is strong as an ox. He was born and raised in New London. His father having been mayor of the city three times. Henry had succeeded his dad in ownership of the family business, Savin Bus Lines. He is a loving, caring, multi-talented individual. I am honored and blessed to have him as a dear friend and as a 'big brother'.

We met through New London Rotary. Shortly after my joining up, Henry and I, along with other club members, attended the District Leaders Conference in White Plains, Westchester County, New York. Following the morning session, the afternoon was designated 'free time'. While most people were heading off to play golf or tennis, Henry and I opted for a walk over to the mall. It was only a short distance from the hotel conference center. During that walk we became acquainted with each other. The man has a treasure trove of knowledge on almost any topic. In fact, Katie and I often said: "Let's ask Henry, he'll know." (Of course, that was in 1988, before I-Phones were providing finger-tip ease and a couple *clicks* away from accessing the internet. But who needs an I-Phone when you have a Henry?)

You see, Henry is a voracious reader and harbors a multitude of varying interests. Most of us going to the library would take out two-three books at a time. He borrows ten or more.

He is an actor and has performed locally with a number of different theater groups, including Mystic Seaport's annual Lantern Light Tours. He has performed in at least one musical, *Fiddler on the Roof.* He has a rich baritone voice that touches one's soul, whether singing or acting. He also narrated the Eastern Connecticut Symphony Orchestra's performance of *Peter and the Wolf* for local school children.

Henry is also a professional story teller. I've had the pleasure of attending a number of his performances, which more often than not are wonderful, poignant Jewish tales from history.

Of course, I'd known of Henry, who was extremely active in the community. He coordinated folk music festivals in New London, and the list continues with his accomplishments. (Someone should write a book about Henry Savin)

***

You can imagine how frustrating and upsetting it was to get home finally and not be able to open the front door with my own key. The dead bolt had been set, which could only be removed from *inside* the house. You see, we always used the front door; but the police officer had gone and secured our home by putting the deadbolt in place – then went and locked the basement door and took the key with him to boot! Pretty efficient, huh?

My sister had been working in the basement runway tending the plants, and apparently had continued on outside to mow the grass. Obviously, the police officer had had to go through our home in order to secure the doors. What were we to do? Call the Waterford Police and ask them to send the officer back with my key?

While the house keys were in my hot little hand and I was jingling them nervously, it finally dawned on me that *I had the home-office key.* So, Henry and I walked around to the back of the house, and we were finally able to enter my home.

Dear Henry was a huge help to me in so many ways. He assisted in tracking down the priest, Father Barry Meehan, who had brought Katie back into the Catholic Church. Katie had left the Church during her college years, while seeking complex answers to life's many complex questions. That very special Father Meehan had been replaced at our church and sent back to Boston College to complete his doctorate studies.

Father Meehan had come all the way from Boston to officiate at Katie's beautiful Mass.

When Henry knew that my good friend Beryl was coming from Maine to be with me, he told me: "Now, Millie, you be sure to have her call me as soon as she arrives."

Doing as I was told, I greeted Beryl upon her arrival with a hug, and informed her she had to call Henry immediately, which she did. As she started speaking with him, he said: "Oh, good, you're there – *she's all yours!*"

We had a much-needed hardy laugh.

I just couldn't thank Henry enough for *all* that he had done for me during so difficult and demanding time. It was during that stressful period when I learned what a *Mitzvah* is in the Jewish Faith. The word Mitzvah in Hebrew means *commandment* and refers to precepts and directives by God … with the additional connotation of one's religious duty. Its secondary meaning in Hebrew (as well as in English) refers to a moral deed performed within a religious duty. It also expresses an individual act of human kindness in keeping with The Law. The expression includes a sense of heartfelt sentiment *beyond* mere legal duty, such as: *"You shall love your neighbor as yourself!"*

***

Before returning to Maine to her family, and to her job, Beryl stayed with me well after Katie's funeral. She was such a huge help during the funeral reception which took place in our home. Beryl made such an impression on everyone, that following her return to Maine, I kept having to answer the same question over and over: *"Who was that lovely lady from Maine?"*

Apparently, in my stupor, I had introduced her only as 'my dear friend from Maine'... without ever having mentioned her name. Brilliant, huh!?

Once Beryl returned to her family in Maine, we stayed in constant touch via email and by phone. We have always been there for each other, and … always will be.

***

My dear neighbors, Tom, Val, and Tristan Ostronic, were just so attentive and helpful to me. They still are – God bless each of them!

Tristan (Tom and Val's son) was sixteen years old and in high school at the time of my dear sister's death. He took it upon himself to call me at least once a week, eventually every other week, to once a month, to check on me and to see if there was anything I needed.

His parents confirmed just how concerned he was for me, due to my being all alone in my own house. It wasn't the first time I'd been alone like that. When we lost Mom, Katie had been working in Hartford then. But now I was really all alone! I recall when Tristan was born, his grandfather would proudly wheel him around in a baby carriage, up-and-down our road.

While in middle school, Tristan learned to play the violin; he ultimately wound up performing with the Waterford High School orchestra. We were all so proud of Tristan! He went off to college, graduated, and has since completed his Executive Master's Degree. Tristan now works as a successful Boston businessman.

To me he is so special – *he is the son I never had.*

***

(We are all absolutely delighted that Tristan has met, courted, and now married the most delightful, charming, fun-loving Rebecca Scholl, M.D. She is an anesthesiologist at Boston Children's Hospital. They are absolutely a beautiful, adoring couple. We wish them the very best in life. We feel it is truly a match made in heaven. God bless them!)

***

Since Katie's passing, the Ostronic Family has included me in their holiday gatherings, treating me as Val's sister. I will always cherish the wonderful times spent with them.

Blessings on all three of my loving and dear friends: Henry, Beryl, and Valerie. Over the many years since Katie's passing, we have become brother and sisters to one another.

***

I was in a state of shock at the loss of Katie. We were extremely close. I was getting all kinds of advice to go for counseling, to seek out support, grieving groups, and so forth. I thought I was doing okay all on my own, but also asked my primary care physician her advice. Since I was now the last of my family line, she agreed that counseling would prove beneficial to me.

I was concerned that whoever the counselor would be might *poo-poo* religion. With my strong faith and the state of mind I was in, I was *not* about to tolerate anyone who failed to respect my faith. That is precisely what was seeing me through so grave a crisis.

Fortunately, my doctor gave me the names of three counselors. The one I chose was warm, compassionate, and understanding. She had grown up Catholic, but had moved away from the church. She had an appreciation for my faith. I really benefitted from our monthly discussions. I found it easy to communicate with her. I actually started with her the beginning of the New Year 2001. The 2000 holiday season was a blur ... it had been challenging, but with help from family and friends, I managed. (I cannot help thinking of the great Beatle piece written by John Lennon and Paul McCarty: *With a Little Help from My Friends.* The lyrics that come to mind are: *Oh, I get by with a little help from my friends.* Thank you, John Lennon and Paul McCarty! Yes, I got by with help from my friends (and family!)

I worked with that counselor – whose name I shamefully cannot remember -- for approximately a year dealing with my loss of Katie. Later that year, as the holidays were once again approaching, she told me that the 2001 Holidays would be even more difficult for me, since in 2000 I was still in a state of shock.

Consequently, I was feeling more apprehensive about that upcoming holiday season. I talked with numerous friends and family in hopes of finding company with whom to share Christmas Eve. However, they *all* had their own plans for that special night. What was I to do? I was feeling very much alone.

I decided I was not going to sit around and mope. I put on my happy face and prepared a special dinner for myself. I set the table (not the kitchen counter) -- with our saved for company-only-dishes featuring broiled medium-rare filet mignon, baked a potato and then slathered it with butter, micro-waved frozen string beans and almonds. For dessert, I dished out a generous portion of Ben & Jerry's Chubby Hubby Ice Cream. Don't you wish you'd been invited too?

Following my delicious meal, I sat, listened to traditional Christmas albums with old favorite soloists such as Bing Crosby crooning his famous "White Christmas"; Julie Andrews with her crystal clear, angelic voice singing, "Away in the Manger" and the "First Noel"; and, of course, the world's favorite tenors: Jose

Carreras singing gloriously "Mary's Boy Child," Placido Domingo's embellishing "Cantique Noel", (also known as O Holy Night), and Luciano Pavarotti always doing justice to "Ave Maria." These three tenors could reach our souls as no others ever could. Who could possibly be sad surrounded by such heavenly voices?

While enjoying the glorious music around me, I read Donna Van Liere's book, "The Christmas Shoes." I also thought back over the years of past Christmas Eves. I then took myself to *Midnight Mass* at ten o'clock with all of its glorious music and magnificent decorations. I walked into the church and was overwhelmed by the number of brilliant red poinsettias set off by white ones. The organist was playing a prelude before the choir encouraged the congregation to join in singing the wonderful old traditional carols.

How I loved the outdoor creche at Saints Peter & Paul Church in Norwich; especially the donkey with its most beautiful facial expression. That outdoor setting was so serene with its wooden creche and natural straw strewn all about the floor. The statues of Mary, Joseph, and Baby Jesus were exquisite.

On Christmas Day I drove to Uncasville, picked-up my cousin Gertrude, and we drove approximately an hour to Rocky Hill, Connecticut to join her sister Grace and her family for dinner. You see, we'd always come together with Mom's family for holidays whether it was Christmas, Easter, Fourth of July, Labor Day, or Thanksgiving. Once Mom and her sisters had all passed, Grace became the family hostess for Thanksgiving and Christmas.

My aunts always had chickens. As a young child, I recall seeing the plucked ones hanging in the cool back hall, just before entering the old homestead. From what I understand, my dad, a city boy, was often called upon to cut the heads off the chickens. I'm glad I didn't have to observe that process of removing the head, followed by the plucking of the feathers.

Our traditional Thanksgiving or Christmas dinners consisted usually of moist roasted turkey (sometimes chicken), giblet gravy,

251

mashed potatoes, squash, turnip, string beans, boiled onions, rolls, butter, and for dessert, a choice of scrumptious homemade pies: pumpkin, apple, or mincemeat.

When it came to certain vegetables, such as squash, my aunts would ask: "Millie, how do you want your squash, with spice or plain?"

My pat answer was always, "I'll have mine plain, please." Consequently, I became known to family and friends as the 'Vanilla Kid'.

Our lifetime custom following holiday meals, whether at my aunts, our home, or at Grace's, was that we all gathered around the organ and sang. Grace's husband Chet played the organ, which he did on that particular occasion. We sang from our John Hancock Christmas Carol Books. (Yes, *John Hancock,* the life insurance company.) We had more than enough of those small, fine print, carol booklets that contained the actual music and accompanying lyrics.

Christmas carols are based on Christian lyrics and relate, in the main, to the Nativity. They were introduced into the church service by St. Francis of Assisi in the Twelfth Century.

At such a Christmas, well before Katie's passing, Grace's husband Chet had shared with me, a piece of music with words that he especially treasured; he thought my first-soprano voice would do it justice: *Little Shepherd Boy.* I gratefully took it along home with me, and the following Christmas sang it as a solo during our church's annual holiday concert. It was so well received that I ended up singing it annually at Mass on Epiphany until I was no longer the cantor. To this day that piece of special music is treasured, not only by me, but by other parishioners. I often get requests to sing it again. Apparently, that glorious piece not only reached my soul, but theirs too.

To this day, Grace and Chet's son, Dan, encourages us to always sing following our holiday dinners. He usually plays the harmonica – one of his many talents. For old times' sake, he brings out the small, tattered John Hancock carol booklets with their

253

finely printed music and words. Because he's so high-tech, along with the rest of his family, we usually have the words on their television, which is conveniently located on the mantle above their huge, gorgeous fireplace. Thank goodness for technology – those of us with aging eyes no longer have to deal with that dreadful tiny print.

***

In January, 2002, when I met with my cherished counselor, she asked, "How were the holidays?"

I answered: "They were *quiet* … but very special to me."

We decided, at that point, I no longer needed her services; but should the occasion arise, I could always call upon her. I'd often thought of her and her profound guidance, but fortunately, never felt the need to call her professionally again. If we ever did meet and recognized each other, we'd welcome it as a breath of fresh air, meeting once more, only this time as *friends*.

During one of our monthly sessions, however, I did discuss with her the initial vision I had had of my dear sister Katie, lying there in that hospital bed, and how it was still haunting me. I just couldn't get over seeing her so ashen and lifeless. I discussed it with my counselor, who recommended thinking, instead, of a joyful time with my sister whenever that scene crept into my mind. What popped into my head immediately was Katie's purchasing and donning of a big, red, straw hat. She had been so ecstatic just to find one that fit!

Katie was approximately six-feet tall (all legs), medium build, big blue-eyes, with brown hair, and a large head -- but not out of proportion -- just difficult in being fitted for hats. (We always had to wear hats to church.) She had reached that height by eighth grade. It made her self-conscious; especially at that early age. She was by far the tallest in her class. She towered over not only the girls, but the boys as well. Just the same, she carried herself well and was highly attractive. Katie was a quiet, conservative, loving person, who also displayed quite an artistic flair.

My dear older sister was a consummate shopper and always knew what was stylish by putting together all the appropriate pieces to create a lovely outfit. In fact, she often surprised me by bringing home outfits earmarked especially for my use. She pretty much became my personal clothing designer. She had beautiful taste in unusual but appropriate styles for her personal banker. I am *not* a shopper. Katie had spoiled little sister by picking out clothes and accessorizing them.

Long after we had become adults, people who hadn't seen us in a long time, and seeing us standing side-by-side, would often say, while looking at Katie, "What happened? You're so tall." Then looking at me, would add: "And you're so ... short."

My pat answer was always the same, while gazing up at my big sister: "She came first and grabbed all the height. I came along later and was tossed the scraps." Yes, I am short.

Over the years, due to my height, I've been called by significantly taller women, a *Lilliputian* – meaning a very small, diminutive person.

My pat answer to that was an old cliche: "Just remember ... dynamite comes in small packages!"

I think we are all familiar with the canned or frozen Green Giant and Le Sueur vegetable brand. The Minnesota Valley Canning Company was founded in 1903 in Le Sueur, Minnesota. The brand *Green Giant Great Big Tender Peas* was first used in 1925; the figure of a giant was introduced three years later by Carly Stanek (Bingum). Consequently, the Green Giant became the mascot. The original mascot was a scowling caveman wearing a bearskin which had very little in common with the familiar green figure of today. In 1935 a young copywriter, Leo Burnett, revised the face of the brand: *he traded the bearskin for a leafy suit, gave the Giant a smile ... and put the word 'Jolly' in front of the Giant's name.*

The Giant made his first television appearance in 1954, and was later voiced by Elmer Dressler, Jr. The booming "Ho! Ho! Ho!" became the Giant's signature tagline in 1961. Since 1972 he has had a young apprentice the Little Green Sprout ... who represents the consumer.

I share all of this with you because, once Katie and I were adults and well beyond our sensitive teenage years, I started calling her, affectionately, the 'Jolly Green Giant' ... and I, the 'Little Green Sprout.' As I mentioned previously, Katie was six-feet tall. I, on the other hand, was only five-foot-three-inches. Needless to say, Katie could pluck items from top shelves that I couldn't even reach without pulling out a step stool.

One more point about Katie. I mentioned her working on bringing plants indoors from their outdoor summer vacation. You see, plants were Katie's *children*. She had had installed in our basement, over an old kitchen table, a grow-light to give her plants just the right amount of daylight and darkness. For example, we've had very good luck with keeping poinsettias from year to year by placing them under that grow-light. They and other plants go outdoors for the summer. Well before the first frost, they come back indoors. While I don't consider myself a gardener, I have continued Katie's 'Annual Ritual.'

I also mentioned that Katie went on to the Hartt College of Music, which became a part of the University of Hartford prior to her graduation. She graduated with a double major in piano and English. She taught piano to young children in the junior program at that university. In addition, she was assistant to the dean for many years.

Katie was a gifted pianist. Our parents gave her a Baby-Grand (approximately five feet in length plus the stool) upon graduating from high school. The rooms in our home are not particularly large; consequently, we've added several additions over the years. Baby-Grand pianos are definitely smaller than Grands (approximately seven feet or more) but took up much more room than a spinet. It finally ended up taking over our dining room with its built-in three-corner china closets. When Katie sat down to play, she could bring to life the soul of the various composers: Mozart, Hayden, Bach, Chopin, and all the other gifted composers. It didn't matter if she was playing a concerto or a sonata. If the piece rose to a brilliant crescendo, tea cups would begin clattering in those china closets. What flourishes of musical brilliance she attained with her strong, slender fingers racing up and down the entire keyboard ... often hand over hand.

Katie and I had been talking about creating a local chapter of the fabled Red Hat Society. This international organization consists of women over age fifty, who would wear purple outfits with gorgeous (often outlandish) red hats. Of course, if women under fifty wanted to join, they were welcome ... but prerequisites deemed they could only wear lavender with pink hats. We had lots of social events, which were always fun.

Fun, pure and simple, was definitely the name of this game and yours truly was the "Queen Mum." We had high teas, went to shows – classic movies, Broadway plays, and other thought-provoking theatrical productions -- or for cocktails with either a small musical combo or featured soloists. We'd sometimes just get together for dinner and for playing games, such as inviting each attendee to search her own handbag looking for certain items, such as lipstick, compact, eyeliner, or a pen and notebook. Usually there were approximately twenty items on that list. Each member searched her own handbag and the items found were placed on the table. Whoever had managed to stuff the most items into her handbag was declared The Champ, and won a prize. The "Queen Mum" presented the prize to the winner, which was always notepaper, or some trinket with a *red hat* on it.

In anticipation of forming our own chapter of the Red Hat Society, Katie and I had shopped for some of our own. She found a gorgeous red straw hat that fit her. Shortly after, dear friends, one of whom was age ninety-eight and her daughter was mid-sixties, were visiting with us. We were talking with them about starting up a Red Hat Chapter. Katie sprang up, dashed off to her room, and grabbed her red hat! She returned to where we were all sitting, donning it with such flair, that it was like Frosty the Snowman coming to life once 'that old black hat was placed upon his head.' It was uncharacteristic of her to be so flamboyant, especially when she threw in a Rosalind Russell flourish, offering her own rendition of "Auntie Mame" from that very special classic film. We all laughed, clapped, and snapped pictures until the film ran out. Moments like these represent the way we have all chosen to remember her, even though she passed away a month later.

Katie's being called home to the Lord prematurely saddened us, as she never got to wear her gorgeous hat in our cherished Red Hat Society. To this day, when I think of Katie, I recall her donning that big magnificent hat with her gorgeous, magnetic smile. That image always brings a smile to me with the warm feeling of being embraced. And it never fails to bring back happier images of Katie as my very own personal shopper. I never wore that hat, it was too large for me, so eventually I gave it to someone who loves hats and would have fun wearing it.

Now my personal shopper was gone. What was I to do? I had to work at not panicking in determining the appropriate accessories for each outfit – especially anything new to the wardrobe. So, I used her bureau for accessories: jewelry, scarves, and so forth. Whenever I bought anything new, I'd walk into my sister's old bedroom and say: "Okay, Katie, what goes with this?" I'd then go to her bureau, open the drawer, and invariably what I needed was right there on top ... *just waiting for me.* You can imagine the warmth that filled me at such moments.

To this day I still get teary-eyed when I hear the Irish song: *I'll Take You Home Again Kathleen.* You see, when Katie was born, Mom wanted a nice Irish name to go with our heritage, Devine. Consequently, our parents named her Kathleen -- a perfect name for a perfect lady.

When Katie passed, I turned to my "Big Brother Henry," and asked him to reach up and retrieve the items that were stored in the small cabinet above the refrigerator. There was no way I could have got hold of those infrequently used dishes stored way up there. In fact, until then, I hadn't even known what Katie had stashed up there.

***

The realization of being the end of my family line made me feel very much alone. Abandoned. However, during my prayer time it came to me that *the Lord does not leave us orphaned.* I also recalled standing alone in my dining room, and gazing towards the heavens, saying to the Lord: "I'm relying on You now -- fully in Your hands." I felt the sudden embrace of a gentle arm around my waist. It had to be Him. From that point on, I gradually picked up the pieces and got my life back on track.

***

As I've mentioned previously, I have not mowed my own lawn since Katie's passing. Thank God for a wonderful landscaping business (Higley's Landscaping, Waterford, Connecticut) that had been mowing for my cousin Gertrude. I called the owner, Alan Higley. He is meticulous, whether he is mowing or plowing. He cares for my property as if it were his own. Alan has trained his workers to do likewise. He and his family have been servicing my landscaping and plowing needs ever since. God bless Alan, his family, and his workers!

***

Katie's sudden demise was one time when having worked in the estate and trust business was too close for comfort for me. My eldest cousin Gertrude and I had settled our aunt's estate in 1975, which also included settling our grandmother's estate from 1945. Katie and I had settled our parents' estates. But Katie's was one I just could not handle. I turned to my attorney and said: "This is one estate *you* need to take care of; just tell me what to do." Which she did.

At some time in our lives, we all experience the loss of someone dear, whether it be people moving away, changing jobs, going off to school, transitioning into the workforce, or losing that special someone who has been called home by the Lord. Transitions like these cause an upset in the balance of our lives. They introduce an element of uncertainty, loss, and apprehension.

As our family diminished, the community became our family. Both Katie and I had been involved in different non-profits, as well as the church. Our actual family of cousins, neighbors, dear friends, and the community were all there for me. God bless each one!

Chapter 11

Career Changes Again

In 2007 following a non-profit board meeting, on which I was serving with Jim Cronin, then president of Dime Bank, he approached me about having lunch. Jim asked if I knew Tom McAvoy; if not, he wanted to introduce him to me. We set a lunch date at the old Bulkeley House on Bank Street in downtown New London. Jim and Tom introduced confidentially the idea of starting a Trust Department at Dime Bank.

I was thrilled with the idea; they wanted my input (at age sixty-five), as a consultant. My having worked for the other bank for approximately thirty-two years, showed me how difficult it was to find a trust company for clients regardless of financial assets. There was a real need then for a local institution that could provide those badly needed, personalized services.

With the support from Dime Bank's board and its management team, Tom McAvoy and I became a unique partnership. With his investment and estate planning knowledge, coupled with my fiduciary background, we worked together from August, 2007 until June, 2008 establishing the necessary policies, procedures, and the department's structure. We actually announced the opening of the Trust Department in April, 2008. That June, I officially became a part-time Trust Officer for the bank.

As it turned out, I had not anticipated the 2008 Recession, so naturally over time my non-profit client business dried up. At that time, non-profits had to concentrate on their current funding and not so much on the future from planned gifts. Fortunately for me, my hours kept increasing with Dime Bank until we reached twenty-hours per week – my limit, not theirs.

When I read the bank's 2007 annual report, which was devoted to all of the bank's outreach to the community, I knew that my joining the Dime Bank was *a heavenly directed match.* (I again attribute this to the Lord's Plan. What wisdom and what wondrous love lay hidden in God's plans.)

That community bank contributes so much to the Eastern Connecticut Region -- not only through its foundation, but through their employees dedicated service. God bless the Blue Crew!

***

When Dime Bank announced the opening of its Trust Department in the spring of 2008, the Marketing Department had decided to take out a billboard on Route 32 in the Uncasville section of Montville, with pictures of Tom McAvoy and me. As I've previously discussed, I belonged to New London Rotary. At that time, the club was assessing fees to members for having their pictures appear in the media outlets, such as newspapers, magazines, church bulletins, etc. – fees ranged a dollar for black-and-white or five dollars for photos in color.

One of our members, at the time, was a New London police officer, who often traveled Route 32 to the two jails in Montville. He had spotted the billboard, with my smiling face and Tom McAvoy's too, and brought it to everyone's attention. I had to go see it for myself! Yes, I took pictures and sent a copy to Beryl. Oh, yes, I paid a handsome fee for that photo to the New London Rotary Club as well.

The billboard was not only on Route 32 where it was very prominent, but also just south of the old deserted Montville Drive-In Theater. It just happened to be near the location of the Wonder Bread and Hostess Cakes Outlet, which was halfway between Norwich and New London. I mention this because after Pop's retirement, Wonder Bread had moved from Norwich to Uncasville. I was particularly moved by the billboard's proximity to that Wonder Bread and Hostess Cakes Outlet. Pop, being a salesman, had a favorite saying: *"He who whispers down a well about the goods he has to sell, will never make as many dollars as he who climbs a tree and hollers."*

After seeing that mammoth billboard, I shared with the bank's president the quote and my interpretation that we were not only *hollering,* but *proclaiming* our great news that we had created this wonderful resource for our community.

270

I remind you that when I moved home, Pop thought working in a bank would be a good job for a young lady. Of course, I felt Pop's blessing on my officially being *back* in banking.

By the time the bank acquired the Trust Department from Guilford Savings Bank effective August 1, 2011, it was time for us to start adding to staff. One of their most capable employees, a paralegal with lots of experience in settling estates and handling trusts, came on board full-time with Dime Bank. She took over the detailed day-to-day administration of trusts and estates; freeing me up to concentrate on bringing in new business, which involved the direct interaction with prospects in reviewing or initiating individual estate plans for them. Tom McAvoy and I often met as a team with these prospects and provided them with a summary of our recommendations, which they could then share with their attorneys.

While working part-time for Dime Bank, I had been keeping Devine Planning going. As I've mentioned, 2007 was the beginning of the 2008 Recession; consequently, my Devine

Planning consulting practice was slowing down. I was accustomed to working with non-profit organizations in helping them to grow their endowments through planned giving; involving not only outright donations, but also clients who might leave bequests, either outright, or via trusts. By the time we reached 2012, my accountant was working on my 2011 income tax return, she approached me about the possibility of closing down Devine Planning (which I did as of June 30, 2012). By that time, I had been in business for over fifteen years.

Our Trust Department personnel worked together as a real team or the proverbial *well-oiled machine.* As I've indicated, the trust business is a detail-oriented and personalized business. There may be similarities in the format of trust and will documents; but, the intricacies of each personal situation make the estate plan unique and customized to that individual. Consequently, one needs to seek legal guidance from estate planning attorneys to do the drafting of such plans.

Needless to say, I have a very strong passion for the trust business and have loved being of service to so many fascinating people throughout all of those fifty-two years. I had a difficult decision to make in deciding to retire at age seventy-five, after working at Dime Bank for a decade. To everyone's astonishment, I actually retired from banking as of September 30, 2017. The hardest part of that decision was knowing I would no longer be working side-by-side with our fabulous trust team, as well as being of assistance to our wonderful clients. With that said, we all still keep in touch by getting together to celebrate our respective birthdays or go out for lunch or cocktails after work. What fun!

We also keep in touch because I have in fact created a revocable living trust. (You'll recall I mentioned this earlier and remind you of its definition: A revocable trust is one for the benefit of the individual who created it, and can be amended or revoked.) I funded it with my home and all of my assets. I am my own trustee for as long as I am *capable*. Hopefully, I'll maintain my sanity and not fall victim to dementia or the dreaded Alzheimer's. In the event

273

of my incapacity during the inevitable aging process, Dime Bank will succeed me as Trustee. In the meantime, that trust department is serving as my agent for the trust's investments, and for my individual retirement account. Dime Bank, therefore, will also serve as Executor & Trustee upon my passing.

***

Let's flash back to when I lived in Boston. We walked all over that great city; but when I moved home, I wasn't doing much in the line of exercising and, therefore, was gaining weight. I learned about Richard Simmons, at that time an exercise guru, and his audio workouts. I did those exercises faithfully every morning for years. I eventually got into walking four to five miles most days; then added workouts at Curves, as well as Zumba, two popular aerobic activities. When Curves in Uncasville closed, I moved on to a gym in Norwich that was about a mile from my bank office. In that way, I could easily stop on my way home; work out, before getting on the interstate highway. When I joined the gym, I also signed up for a personal trainer once per week, which was very good. When that trainer left to take another job, I decided to sign with a new trainer, twice per week, and have been doing so since December, 2015.

I find working with my personal trainer, David Giles, *invaluable*. He knows how to adjust my workout so I maximize the benefit, no matter if I'm feeling great or having an off day, or dealing with a broken bone in my foot, or my sprained neck. David is extremely knowledgeable and flexible. He shows me what to do. He never starts a session with me without first asking, "How are you feeling today?"

In July, 1999 when I started with a new primary care physician, I was diagnosed with adult-onset type two Diabetes, which scared the living daylights out of me. Up until that diagnosis, all I had ever heard about were the horrors of that disease: having to inject insulin, possible amputations; need I go on …

At that time, Joslin Clinic was just opening a facility at Lawrence + Memorial Hospital. My primary care physician sent me there to meet with a diabetes nurse-educator and a nutritionist. Thanks to that training and a subsequent refresher, I've been controlling my diabetes with diet and exercise ever since. I take no medication for it, and have not taken any since that initial diagnosis. I test my glucose daily and try my best to eat everything in moderation.

Once I really got involved with exercising, and it became a focus for me to maintain my health, I thought back to my dad and remembered how strong and slim he was while working for Wonder Bread. (Remember that famous catch phrase: "Helps build strong bodies twelve ways!") He was always jumping on and off the bread truck throughout the day, making his deliveries while carrying heavy trays of bread or Hostess Twinkies into the stores or restaurants. When he retired, although he tried to exercise, he was not doing so in a formal program. Therefore, I think the lack of the amount of exercise he had been doing might be attributed to our losing him approximately a year after his retirement.

***

During all of these many years, I can assure you, Millie has *not* been all work and no play. I've had the good fortune to do a lot of traveling over the years. Growing up, our parents made sure we took road trips to all of the New England states, plus New York, New Jersey, and the Washington, D.C. area, as well as Canada.

The year after pop died, Mom, Katie, and I vacationed in Hawaii: a beautiful and colorful place that none of us had visited previously. You can imagine, in June, when trees and flowers are finally blooming in New England, flying home from Oahu to JFK Airport in New York, things appeared very drab and dull. This lack of color hit us, especially after being surrounded by gorgeous flowering shrubs such as bougainvillea; meals served with small purple orchids and orange nasturtiums decorating the dishes. It didn't matter if it was breakfast, lunch, or dinner, each serving had

277

these gorgeous, edible blooms decorating the plates – so festive, bright, and colorful.

One of the first trips I took all on my own was in the 1970s. Between working full-time (tax-season was an extremely busy time for those of us in the trust department), and studying for my bachelor's degree, as well as community involvement, it was difficult to take time off. I was definitely in need of a break. So, I talked with the boss; we determined a good time would be a Tuesday to Tuesday in early March. With blessings from the boss, I went to see a travel agency, just down the street from the bank. I informed them of my availability and with a big smile asked, "Now, where can I go?" We both chuckled.

The agent told me about a Single World Cruise to Cancun and Cozumel, Mexico, along with some other ports in the Caribbean that were available on those dates. We booked it, then and there.

I took a chance on who my roommate would be, but specified both a female and a non-smoker. I figured that we wouldn't be spending much time in the cabin ... just for showering and sleeping. My assigned roommate Diana was a lovely person, in her thirties, like me. She was also in business, enjoyed reading, and was a similar personality to mine.

It turned out there were ten of us who had booked with Single World – two men and eight women. The first night on board the ship, we met our tour director and became acquainted with each other over cocktails and dancing. Those two men certainly had their exercise that evening as they made a point of dancing with each of the women from our group. In fact, Gary and I won a prize for endurance on the dance floor. We each received a prize of a key chain with the ship's logo.

You'll recall my description of Loretta Young, who was very graceful and charming, who always swirled as she entered the room with her skirt a flair. I loved to dance and especially the twirling. As a child, I took tap dancing lessons. I'll never forget the catchy jingle we learned to begin our lesson:

"First you put your two knees close up tight, then you swing them to the left, and then swing them to the right. Step around the floor kind of nice and light, then twist around, twist around, with all your might."

Gary must have also enjoyed dancing. He was tall, thin, with dark hair, and a good dancer – easy to follow. Then there was Glen who enjoyed music but basically had two left feet. He just swayed back and forth – not moving far from the start. He was an engineer, a little on the stocky side, with an air about him that made him difficult to get to know.

In addition to Diana, the other women in our group were quite unique.

Kitty, a vivacious, fun-loving gal who was the life of the party; Angela who was strikingly beautiful, a little more reserved, but very pleasant; Maggie, a little on the stocky side, shiest of the group, but always pleasant; Kelly, slim and attractive but seemed a little scatter-brained; Adele, very serious, reserved, and enjoyed reading – nose always in a book; Georgia, another vivacious individual with lots of spunk and full of fun; and Susan (Sue) who was athletic and loved to swim.

Our whole group of ten were in the thirties and forties. We all got along nicely; but to my knowledge, no lasting relationships.

Our tour director offered us an optional trek upon arrival in Cancun, Mexico. We would take a smaller boat from the pier where the cruise ship had docked. This smaller boat, with a glass bottom, would take us snorkeling to see all of the beautiful coral.

Snorkeling is the practice of swimming on or through a body of water while equipped with a diving mask, a shaped breathing tube called a snorkel, and usually swim fins. This limited equipment allows the snorkelers to observe underwater life in a natural setting for extended periods, with relatively little effort and breathe while face down on the surface. It's a popular recreational activity, particularly in tropical locations. The primary appeal is the limited gear one needs versus all of the equipment and training required for scuba diving.

Following the stop for those who wanted to snorkel in the crystal-clear aquamarine water, this boat would then take us to a small island, Isla Majures, off the coast of Cancun, where we would have a picnic lunch, swim, and play volleyball. It all sounded like great fun. We were all looking forward to the exercise and competition in our volleyball game.

Diana and Glen chose to stay behind and sightsee or shop. Gary and the rest of us decided to take this optional tour. Six of us, including Gary, went snorkeling while Angela and I remained on the glass-bottomed boat and were amazed by what we saw … absolutely gorgeous, colorful coral. The snorkelers were also delighted with their sojourn.

Once everyone was again onboard, our motor boat revved its engine and we headed off to that small island, Isla Majures. It was a very pretty little island with a dazzling white sands beach. It was set up for us to picnic and to enjoy a game of volleyball to which we were all looking forward – but, as we had been forewarned, it offered *no* shopping opportunities.

Upon arrival, the crew threw the anchor over the side of the boat. Lo and behold, the *rope* slipped right through their hands. The anchor sank to the bottom of the ocean. One of the young native well-built crew members stripped off his shirt immediately and dove into the water in search of it. He surfaced. No luck! Still in the water, he discussed with his comrades what to do. Another muscled member of the crew dove in – again, no luck finding that elusive anchor. They then decided they better radio *the boss* for help, who sent a truck to pick up a spare anchor and load it onto another boat that brought it to us. This unfortunate episode took a good hour or more.

Once we were anchored securely, which was offshore, we had to disembark the boat by getting into the water, then follow the tow-rope to shore. Poor Angela, who had at one point in her life come close to drowning, was beginning to panic; since she didn't know how to swim and feared going into the water. She was so scared. We all felt for her. This was an unexpected detail most of us were not expecting. She had taken this excursion thinking we'd be brought up to the dock.

God bless that crew who came to her rescue. They escorted her to shore. Much to her surprise, she made it with her life-preserver on and with their help, while holding on to the tow-rope. By the time she returned to the boat, she sighed with relief: "I made it!" This was a revelation for her: the beginning of her facing and overcoming her fear of the water.

Obviously, due to the delay in getting us ashore, having our picnic lunch, and getting back onboard that boat, there was no time for volleyball. We were all disappointed at not being able to play and work off some of our energy and frustration.

I mentioned that we were in Mexico. There was also a time difference of an hour. Unfortunately, our tour director hadn't adjusted her watch to get us back to the ship on time. By the time we arrived, the ship had sailed. The farther out it got, *our vessel was getting smaller and smaller*. Someone on the dock, with whom the tour director had spoken, told her he had radioed the ship, which was sending a tender (a smaller boat that ferries people and supplies between ship and shore) for us. We waited about a half-hour and didn't see any sign of a boat coming for us. We were stranded. How do we get ourselves out of this "fine kettle of fish?"

Fortunately, including the tour guide, there were nine of us. If I'd been by myself, I would have been panicking. We put our heads together and decided the best thing to do was to go to the police. Our next challenge was to communicate with the officer. He spoke no English; we spoke no Spanish.

With our hands, we motioned for a piece of paper and a writing utensil, then drew a picture of a big ship, with its name printed on it while leaving the pier; then we drew stick figures of people on the dock. We were able finally to communicate our dilemma that nine of us had missed the ship … left behind … deserted.

The officer radioed the captain and the response was: "Tell them to take a taxi to the airport and to fly to Cozumel, then get to Playa del Carmen, the port where they will join the tender picking up the passengers who had been touring the ruins in Cozumel. All those passengers would then board that boat and be taken to the ship."

In the meantime, the captain announced to the entire ship that there were nine of us who had *missed the boat*. He asked the other passengers to be kind to us when we boarded the ship, because the cruise company didn't want to discourage us from traveling with them again. In the meantime, Glen and Diana, who had not joined us in the excursion, had figured out *we* were the eight people plus the tour guide who had been left behind.

Since there were nine of us, we had to get two cabs from the pier and travel to the airport. Mind you, most of our little group were wearing bathing suits. We made quite a sight for the fliers on business trips going between destinations.

Once at the airport, we started pulling out credit cards, that is: those of us who had brought them with us. Few had anticipated needing such cards, nor passports on this tiny island in Mexico. The realization hit most of us that many folks had left either credit cards or passports in safes *aboard the ship*. If they had credit cards, they had pretty much maxed them out. This fiasco held true for our tour director as well.

That morning, I had had quite a debate with myself prior to leaving the ship: "Do I take my credit cards and passport or do I put them in the ship's safe? After all we will be in Mexico."

I was very glad that I had brought both with me. Being a banker, I was able to come to the rescue with *my* credit card and covered the fees for all nine of us to fly to the designated Porta de Carmen where we would meet the tender. (At that point, I didn't care about cost ... just get me back on that ship!) The tour guide assured me that I'd be reimbursed once we were aboard the ship ... which she honored.

In the meantime, our captain was *not* happy with that tour director. He read her the proverbial "riot act" in no uncertain terms! Fortunately, the rest of our cruise was uneventful. We made sure in each port we visited to return to the ship in plenty of time before the designated sailing time.

Meanwhile, I was chuckling to myself, and couldn't wait to get back to the office and tell them that we had missed the ship. They all knew that I was always prompt. Beryl Hobart and I were raised in such a way, that if you were five minutes early, you were already late. Consequently, we always tried to be *ten* minutes early for any appointments.

Once home, I shared our story with the office crew. As I began to laugh, the others joined in, with the boss giving me a reproachful look. To this day, I chuckle about that zany misadventure.

***

Speaking of adventures, another dear, bodacious and financial friend, Laura Berry, shared special times and events with me. As an investment advisor, her special focus was investing in socially responsible companies. She is approximately ten years younger than me, and lost her brother a year ahead of my losing my sister. We are both Catholic, sharing our faith and visits to faith-filled events, indoors and out -- such places as the Madison, Connecticut *Mercy by the Sea Retreat & Conference Center,* which has a labyrinth, as described by Episcopal Priest Laura Artreso, who is also an author and a speaker says: "A labyrinth ... a walking meditation, a path of prayers, and a blueprint where Psyche meets Spirit."

Laura and I actually joined forces and bid on a Hot-Air-Balloon Ride during a non-profit fund-raising silent auction in May, 1998. It turned out that we were the successful bidder. We met the dapper, generous, and gracious balloon pilot that evening to arrange for our special trip to take place in August, 1998. Wouldn't you know it, I had the misfortune of falling and fracturing my ankle in early June. Ouch – a real bummer! In spite of my wise doctor having told me I'd be ready to go for it that August, the caring and thoughtful pilot was leery, rightfully so. He warned us that sometimes the landing can be rough. He didn't want me to reinjure the ankle. That made good sense to us. I certainly didn't want any repercussions from this exciting excursion.

Fortunately, we took the pilot's advice and postponed until Saturday of Memorial Day Weekend in 1999. It was definitely an adventure. Just getting into the basket alone, more properly known as the gondola, was a challenge for me with my short legs. Not my most graceful maneuver. I hadn't realized that there was a *toe hole* in the gondola to reach for, about halfway down the side of it. In fact, I ended up almost doing a non-graceful acrobatic split before bringing my other leg in with me. I'm sure it was a sight to behold with one leg sticking straight up out of the gondola, and gravity helping me with the other in reaching the base of the basket. I was extremely glad that we had waited for this awesome trip.

By the time my whole body was included, the top of the basket reached my waist. I couldn't help thinking about my very tall sister, had she not had an aversion to heights, and been interested in joining us, the gondola might have reached the top of her long legs – maybe even her hips. She would have been afraid of falling out. Laura and I being height-deprived are approximately the same size. We were comfortable in the gondola. My sister Katie would definitely have been cramped.

The handsome and serene pilot took us up at six o'clock in the morning, as part of the Bristol, Connecticut Balloon Festival. They generally schedule these flights at that time of year between five and six in the morning and six to seven in the evening, when the air currents are calm. Weather is a very important factor in hot-air-ballooning safely. Winds, both on the ground and aloft, temperature, pressure systems, rain, and fog all play crucial roles in a pilot's decision to fly, or not. Most commercial ride companies require passengers to call-in the day before a flight to check weather conditions. If a flight is canceled due to weather, "sky drifters," as the pilots are called, will reschedule the flight for another day, or may offer a refund if another day is not available. Safety of everyone involved is critically important in planning such awesome adventures.

We were extremely lucky, as it turned out to be an absolutely gorgeous, gloriously crystal-clear day. We floated just above the tree line, just beyond "our reach," as we glided over the hills and dales of several towns in the hour that we were aloft – no tethering for us. We heard birds chirping – but not much else, except for the *whoosh* of the hot air into the balloon to keep us afloat. One very special moment was hovering above the calm waters of the Farmington, Connecticut Reservoir. At that point, the debonair, thoughtful pilot, with a gentleman's wink calmly lowered the gondola to give us the full image of the balloon's reflection. Its strong cables held the gondola beneath it, with just the three of us in it. One almost felt like *Jonathan Livingston Seagull* soaring through the atmosphere with a bird's eye view taking in the magnificent beauty and calmness surrounding us.

292

While in the air, we could look down and see the *chase vehicle* keeping up with us. Doubtless, you're wondering what a chase vehicle is. While it is certainly possible to enjoy the sport of hot-air-ballooning without the presence of a chase vehicle, returning from the landing site by foot or hitch hiking, many balloonists opt to be followed by their ground crew in some sort of vehicle. Crew at the landing site can aid with the landing itself, by catching a drop-line and guiding the balloon out of a tight space; or with extracting the balloon system from a remote location, such as deep in a farmer's field; and with packing up all of the equipment. The pilot had vigilant scouts who meticulously kept track of where we were, and remained available should anything go awry.

Gazing down, we found the chase car, an older Ford station wagon, in itself fascinating, because we were not following any particular street map. As our trip was ending, our conscientious pilot asked us to be alert and to warn him if we saw any potentially dangerous sights. He carefully guided the balloon, as he released its air, thus avoiding high-tension lines while seeking an open field. We glided down landing gently, in a field of tall grass that was just off a business parking lot in Wethersfield, Connecticut. As we landed, our dashing, handsome pilot gave us a snappy salute. The eager crew arrived just as we were landing, and hustled to grab the drop-line to guide our gondola to the edge of the parking lot. The people arriving for work that Saturday morning had their entertainment, watching us land, especially with the big old black Ford wagon pulling into their parking area.

The delightful crew greeted us with a traditional champagne toast upon landing. Legend has it that early French aeronauts carried champagne to appease frightened spectators at the landing sites ... sometimes even angry ones.

After our most welcomed champagne toast, the crew and pilot gathered up all of the gear, and drove us back to the Bristol Fairgrounds. It was an awesome opportunity: one I've treasured ever since. Yes, I would do it again if such a chance were ever to arise ... just to experience the world as the birds do. Once simply was not enough!

Another tradition among balloonists involves reciting "The Balloonists Prayer" before a hot-air-balloon flight. There is also a slightly modified version that is intended as part of the post-flight ceremony. While the exact origin and author are unknown, it is believed to have been adapted from an old Irish sailor's blessing from long ago:

Recited BEFORE Flight

May the winds welcome you with softness.
May the sun bless you with its warm hands.
May you fly so high and so well
That God joins you in laughter
And sets you gently back again
Into the loving arms of Mother Earth.

Recited AFTER Flight

The Winds have welcomed you with softness.
You have flown so high and so well
That God has joined you in your laughter
And set you gently back again
Into the loving arms of Mother Earth.

Yes, indeed, I would go up again just to have God join me in laughter!

***

The summer of 2000 brought to New London twenty-two Class A glorious and spectacular Tall Ships from all over the world. Some of those ships included, the Amerigo Vespucci from Italy, (A side tidbit of history: Amerigo Vespucci, 1454-1512, was an Italian merchant, explorer, and navigator from the Republic of Florence, from whose name the terms America and Americas are derived.) Bluenose II from Canada, Danmark from Denmark, Dar Mlodziezy from Poland, Esmeralda from Chile, Juan Sebastian de Elcano from Spain, Libertad from Argentina, and many more. All part of the Op Sail Festival. While in port, the crew permitted everyone the opportunity to explore these massive, grand ships.

Katie and I were blessed to be aboard one of the viewing vessels at the beginning of the parade of ships, led by our own *Flagship of the Festival,* United States Coast Guard Barque Eagle – truly awesome!

The Coast Guard Barque, *Eagle* is a 295-foot barque (a type of sailing vessel with three or more masts and main-masts rigged square) used as a training cutter for future officers of the United States Coast Guard. She is only one of two active commissioned sailing vessels in the United States military today, along with the USS Constitution, which is ported in Boston Harbor.

Each summer, the Eagle deploys with cadets from the United States Coast Guard Academy and candidates from the Officer Candidate School. The time aboard ranges from a week to two months. Yes, it is used for training the cadets and officer candidates; but the ship also performs a public relations role, not only for the Coast Guard, but for the United States as well.

Are you aware that our Barque Eagle was originally the *Horst Wessel,* one of three sail-training ships of the German Navy, pre-World War II? It was built in Hamburg, Germany in 1936. The gorgeous vessel was taken as war reparations by the United States. It was re-commissioned the U. S. Coast Guard Cutter Eagle and sailed to New London, Connecticut, which has been her permanent homeport ever since.

In 1972, at the request of the West German government, the Eagle returned to Germany for the first time since 1946, and visited the port of Kiel, where she had formerly moored on numerous occasions as Horst Wessel. While there, she participated in a five-day race against Gorch Fock II: Germany's replacement for the actual sister ship to the Eagle. We were delighted to see that even the German Tall Ship *Gorch Fock II* came and visited its kindred, our Barque Eagle, formerly the German ship *Horst Wessel*.

Have you ever wondered what it would be like to climb the rigging of one of those Tall Ships? The open netting of ropes and wires needing to be climbed in order to unfurl and to stow the mammoth sails. I cannot begin to imagine doing that, especially at sea with uncalm waters rocking the ship. It *might* be a possibility for me, if in port … where the ship is anchored at a pier. Believe me, doing it is not on my *Bucket List*.

I've heard sailors describe the adrenalin buzz as huge, even having done it before. The amount of courage to work aloft in any weather has not been diminished much over the centuries by the introduction of modern safety harnesses. I understand that you climb free, hand over hand, without being clipped on; it is only when you step onto the foot ropes and go out on to the yard to stow sails, that one clips the safety harness to a wire jackstay. By being clipped to the safety harness, one is free to use his hands to stow the sail.

Perhaps you've never seen sailors climbing those treacherous riggings. If not, you should watch the movie *Treasure Island* with Charlton Heston, based on Robert Louis Stevenson's classic adventure.

As these magnificent Tall Ships paraded into New London's harbor, the masts were lined with their sailors – very impressive sights. We were glad we didn't have to climb those riggings to the heights they had to go on the masts. Proudly – we saluted our men and women in blue.

In addition to all of the Class A (all square-rigged vessels: barque, barquentine, brig, brigantine, or ship rigged and all other vessels more than 131 feet length overall), we also had in port at that time numerous Class B (traditionally rigged vessels: gaff rigged sloops, ketches, yawls, and schooners, less than 131 feet in length.) A good example of a Class B is the *Spirit of Bermuda,* which is a modern-built Bermuda sloop. She is a replica of a Royal Navy sloop-of-war, depicted in a well-known 1831 painting. The Bermuda Sloop was a type of small sailing ship built in Bermuda between the seventeenth and nineteenth centuries. She is fitted with a gaff rig, a combination of gaff and square rig, known as the "Bermuda rig." This type of sloop was used by Bermudian merchants, privateers, and other seafarers.

In addition, Class C vessels very similar to Class B, but not carrying spinnaker-like sails, participated as well. Spinnakers are large triangular sails set forward of all the other sails, used by racing and cruising yachts when churning downwind, meaning in whatever direction the wind is blowing.

That 2000 Op Sail Festival of Tall-Ships was truly memorable and spectacular!

***

As a trust officer, I needed to maintain my certifications through continuing education. In December, 2001 I opted to take a Caribbean Cruise on the Holland America *Volendam*. I had chosen that particular trip to attend Louis Rukeyser's investment sessions while at sea. At that time, Louis Rukeyser was known as the *investment guru,* given his weekly public broadcasting TV shows. While at sea, we listened to him, and to his colleagues, as they lectured on investments. Once in port, we were released delightfully to do whatever we desired. Often it included sightseeing.

***

Another delightful adventure was the Antebellum Cruise on the Intracoastal Waterway from Charleston, South Carolina to Jacksonville, Florida. I so enjoyed visiting Beaufort and Savannah,

Georgia, with their gorgeous mansions and banyan trees with Spanish moss appearing to be dripping from them. The tour also visited Jekyll Island before reaching our destination of Jacksonville. I stayed an extra night in Jacksonville in order to rent a car and drive down to St. Augustine, which is just brimming with Native and Colonial history and so utterly gorgeous.

Of course, I had to tour the Castillo de San Marcos, the oldest masonry fort in the continental United States. Nine wooden fortifications, designed to protect St. Augustine, were burned by invaders. This large Spanish stone fortress was built in 1672 by Spain's militia. It took twenty-three years to complete. The fortress was built using *coquina* as the building material, a stone-like compound made of shell and limestone.

This mighty fortress *was never taken in battle* and played a pivotal role in protecting Spanish St. Augustine from the 1700s to the late 1800s.

***

Another dear friend, Jeane Haggerty Swatzburg, and I took a weekend cruise from *Boston to No Where*, which was so relaxing and delightful – just what we needed. Jeane and I first met while working for Hartford National Bank and traveled to banking conventions together. We went with four other friends (two married couples) on that cruise in October, 2011. It was during that cruise when we had the late October snowstorm that hit Boston, Providence, and inland Connecticut. It was fascinating to watch snow falling on the open sea. By the time we were back on shore, riding back to Providence to pick up our car, the roads were all fine … for us. But one couple, who lived in Tolland, Connecticut, was greeted with eight inches of snow upon arriving back at home.

There were a couple of other big trips planned but they had to be canceled due to hurricanes that closed airports before we could get out of their way. Thank God for cancellation insurance.

Chapter 12

Caught by the Traveling Bug

After Mom had died, Katie and I decided our first trip would be to Ireland ... since Pop was both Irish and Scottish. We'd always heard about grandparents coming over *from the old country* ... sailing from Galway. Consequently, we made our first trip a two-week tour of Ireland in late June, 1983. We flew into Shannon

Airport and began our glorious tour. Literally, it struck us that we had seemingly stepped back in time by a good twenty years.

Of course, the tour introduced our taste buds to scones with clotted cream – scrumptious! At lunch time, we were encouraged to enjoy the offerings from the pubs or tea rooms. These venues provided fabulous delicacies, and at reasonable prices too. Even our breakfasts and dinners were included in the cost of the tour.

The tea rooms also introduced us to Irish Tea, which delighted my taste buds. And my happy taste buds decided for the rest of the trip that's what I would drink rather than coffee. I wasn't use to the strong coffee offered abroad – it was just too bitter for me … not enough sugar could be added to satisfy my taste. As I've previously mentioned, I've always been referred to as '*The Vanilla Kid*' by my family and close friends since I don't enjoy a lot of spices nor strong coffee. Just mentioning strong coffee, my body shudders. In fact, as a child I would often say, "I'll have mine plain, please."

We were intrigued by all the little cottages with their thatched roofs. In fact, I actually was given the opportunity to see the inside of a private home – simple and basic … very humbling. Many years later, when my cousin and I visited Ireland, while touring the British Isles, those cottages' thatched roofs, for the most part, had been replaced with more standardized materials. If you've ever had to replace a roof, you know there is a wide variety in shingles: cedar, asphalt, enviro-shingles, to name a few. Thatched roofs are difficult and expensive to maintain, unlike the more modern materials. The cost for replacing was prohibitive. The Irish government had provided grants to homeowners to replace them with modern roofing. Today you see these specialty roofs preserved only on historic buildings.

By the time we reached Galway, you know Katie and I had to go put at least our hands in the legendary Galway Bay. It was that area from where immigrants, including our grandparents, had sailed to the United States … especially during the Great Irish Potato Famine (1845-1849, which returned in 1879.) That natural event was caused by a potato blight, which infected potato crops throughout Europe. The blight was a disease that destroyed both the leaves and the edible roots (or tubers) of the potato plant. This Potato Famine also caused some one-hundred-thousand deaths outside Ireland and influenced much of the unrest in the widespread European Revolutions of 1848. From 1846, the impact of that blight was exacerbated by the Whig government's economic policy of laissez-faire capitalism. (An economic doctrine that opposed either governmental regulation or interference in commerce; *noninterference* in affairs of others.) Longer-term causes included the system of absentee landlordism, and single-crop dependence.

Over the years, whether or not we've recognized it, we've all seen the results of absentee landlords, owners of often derelict, multi-family houses, and single-crop dependence affecting our own country, as well as others. In the early nineteenth century, however, tenant farmers as a class, especially in western Ireland, struggled to provide for themselves, so did the British Market with cereal crops. (Cereal crops are any grass that produces an edible grain, such as oats, rye, wheat, rice, or maize.) Many farmers had long existed at virtually the subsistence economic level given the small sum of their meager wages -- as well as the various hardships that the land presented for farming in some regions.

The famine was a watershed in the history of Ireland, which from 1801 to 1922 was ruled directly by Westminster as part of the United Kingdom of Great Britain and Ireland. That famine and its effects permanently changed the island's demographic, political, and cultural landscape. It produced an estimated two million refugees and created a century-long population decline.

As a result of all of this unrest, Irish families came in droves to the welcoming shores of the United States of America to join family members who had previously settled in our own beautiful country. These people arrived at the infamous Ellis Island, the stopping point for all immigrants, and were greeted by our gorgeous Statue of Liberty, as had the Bodenwein Family upon arrival from Germany, with Emma Lazarus' sonnet:

"Give me your tired, your poor,
Your huddled masses yearning to breathe free,
The wretched refuse of your teeming shore.
Send these, the homeless, tempest-tossed to me,
I lift my lamp beside the golden door!"

By the time we reached Ireland in 1983, it was no wonder we sensed that twenty-year step-back in time. It was truly an eye-opening moment for us. What our grandparents had had to experience before leaving that beautiful home country. It made us think about our parents and their families having lived through the Great Depression and what they'd experienced just to survive. Boxing buffs will no doubt agree that a good example of the hardships endured by families during our Great Depression can be seen in the famous movie: *Cinderella Man* (Russell Crowe) as James J. Braddock.

That visit to Ireland was humbling, emotional, and yet heart-warming by what we saw. The Irish are beautiful, loving, caring, welcoming people.

In our trek through that gorgeous countryside, we were so impressed by the green Connemara Marble and the three-hundred-sixty-degree view from the Hill of Tara. It was there that no matter where we looked, it was *green* – at least forty different shades of green. It was truly a magnificent vista!

It was in a Dublin pub where I ended up singing a solo. The pianist was encouraging someone from the audience to sing the beautiful old piece: *Oh, Danny Boy.* No one was volunteering, so I did. Of all pieces to sing in Ireland! I surprised myself by being able to sing it and not break into tears. You see that piece had been played at Pop's funeral and was so close to my heart. It was my loving tribute to him, to his family, and to all they had endured.

Oh, yes, I did kiss the Blarney Stone, which was quite the adventure; climbing to the top of that castle, lying on your back, while stretching your neck, and extending your lips to kiss that stone. Thank goodness there was an attendant to help you and to warn you to remove loose jewelry before lying back. The Irish children would gather below that stone at the base of the castle in hopes of pocketing loose change or other treasures they could sell.

Since our village of Quaker Hill is within the town of Waterford, you know that we were delighted to visit *Waterford, Ireland.* And we, of course, toured the Waterford Crystal Factory. They made such gorgeous and often unique crystal pieces, having won numerous shows. In fact, when the Crystal Mall was built in Waterford, Connecticut, the management had hung a magnificent Waterford crystal chandelier in the center of it. At the invitation of our then First Selectman, Thomas Sheridan, who had been born in Ireland, the Mayor of Waterford, Ireland also even came for the mall's dedication.

Katie and I enjoyed that tour so much, that our next adventure was a two-week tour of England. It took us from London with all of its magnificence, history, and treasures, to all around that beautiful country. The highlight to us was the gorgeous and serene Lake District of northwestern England. It was also the home of poet William Wordsworth (1770-1850). After all we did grow

311

up with those classic literary treasures. Aunt Trudy had been an English teacher and made sure we had good books to read. And part of Katie's double major was English.

We were enthralled by the Lake District and by Wordsworth's home area which brought back many similar memories Katie and I had shared from our home being surrounded by woods and pine groves, which we loved exploring. He was a fascinating individual and such a treasure with his literary contributions. I share this with you briefly from his biography:

By the age of thirteen, Wordsworth had lost both parents. As an orphan, he was sent by his guardian to a grammar school at Hawkshead in the heart of the Lake District. There, he received an excellent education in classics, literature, and mathematics. The chief advantage for him, while there, was a chance to indulge in the boyhood pleasures of living and playing outdoors.

As one who grew up exploring the great outdoors with my sister, we so appreciated his description of the natural scenery, which can *terrify* as well as nurture us. I recall one sunny winter day, ground covered with snow, when Katie and I decided to go for a walk in the woods. I remind you that Katie was much taller and four years older than me. We were trudging along and at one point decided to climb to the top of the long stone wall rather than keep plodding up through the snow. By the time we reached the abrupt end of that wall, it was surrounded by deep water, a combination of melting ice and snow and an overflowing pond. Katie, with her long legs, could have stepped down into that water and probably been just fine. However, with my short legs, had I done so, I would have been virtually wading through it and soaked to the bone. We knew better than to return home soaking wet in the middle of winter. Consequently, we ended up turning around and retracing our steps back to the beginning of that stone wall and avoiding further trouble. We never told our parents about that little excursion.

One never knows what you might find while traveling through the woods. There could be beautiful discoveries such as a clump of pure white delicate Indian pipes, or magnificent coral-colored-lady slipper plants; or you could wind up walking on a trail, finding arrow heads that most likely had been used with bows and arrows. Of course, one could always come upon a snake, basking on a rock or coiled in your path, right where you were about to plant your foot. Never mind the variety of large and small beetles and bugs. While Katie was terrified of snakes, and I was not enamored with hornets nor bees, she treasured being outside. I was much happier *indoors*.

Wordsworth testified to the beauty and fears one experiences in the forests: "I grew up fostered alike by beauty and fear." Its' generally benign aspect gave this growing boy the inspiration for one of his grandest literary works: *Lines Composed a Few Miles Above Tintern Abbe* ... and the unforgettable quote, "... Nature never did betray the heart that loved her."

We enjoyed that tour so much that we planned another trip for a two-week tour of Scotland. Again, the contrasts of the countryside from the cities were magnificent. But what I remember most in Edinburgh: the memorial to the Skye Terrier, referred to as the 'Greyfriars Bobby.' This amazing dog *guarded his master's grave for fourteen years* in the 19th Century. There is a fabulous book by that name, written by Eleanor Atkinson in 1912. Disney's movie, released in 1961, tells the true story based on that book. Edinburgh has a beautiful statue in tribute to that dear, loving, devoted dog.

We truly enjoyed the moderate pace of the two-week tours because we saw and learned a lot, while at a relatively relaxed pace. We enjoyed mostly the interaction with the people of whichever country we visited. Each of these tours gave us a true feeling for that particular land and its customs. We found traveling fascinating, educationally exhilarating, and most enjoyable.

Katie and I squeezed in a trip to Bermuda in October, 1987. It turned out that trip was immediately following a hurricane that had swept the island. In spite of the mounds of debris everywhere, we got to enjoy a lot of tennis on beautiful courts that were surrounded by gorgeous flower gardens, not to mention the overall beauty of the island and its gorgeous landscapes.

In 1990, Katie and I had driven to Scarboro, Ontario, Canada to visit a dear friend I had met through the National Secretaries Association in the late 1960s. We traveled all over the area, including a trip to the awesome Niagara Falls. If you've never been to see them, they are well worth the trip. They are so spectacular that many honeymooners have made them their destination.

Niagara Falls is a group of three waterfalls at the southern end of Niagara Gorge, spanning the border between the United States' state of New York and the Canadian province of Ontario. The largest of the three falls is Horseshoe Falls, also known as Canadian Falls, which straddles the border between the United States and Canada. The smaller American Falls and Bridal Veil Falls lie entirely within the United States.

These magnificent falls are located on the Niagara River, which drains Lake Erie into Lake Ontario. The combined falls have the highest flow rate of any waterfall in North America that has a vertical drop of more than fifty meters (just over one-hundred-fifty feet).

Niagara Falls was formed when glaciers receded at the end of the Wisconsin glaciation (the last ice age), and water formed Great Lakes, which carved a path through the Niagara Escarpment en route to the Atlantic Ocean.

In June of 1990 we visited the falls; it was a crystal clear, sunny day. As we approached the falls from the parking area, you could hear their mighty roar. The nearer we got, they drowned out conversation, so one simply basked in the beauty of their mist. We actually got to see a gorgeous rainbow generated by the sun's hitting the spray from the Horseshoe Falls. We did not opt for the available boat trip beneath the falls, which I understand is a phenomenal one … although one should definitely wear rain gear.

We spent the night in the area known as Niagara-on-the-Lake, which gave us the opportunity to enjoy its theater's hilarious

317

live production of Shakespeare's *The Merry Wives of Windsor,* also referred to as *Sir John Falstaff and the Merry Wives of Windsor.* It is a comedy by William Shakespeare, first published in 1602, though believed to have been written about 1597. The storyline takes place in the town of Windsor, also the location of the royal Windsor Castle in Berkshire, England. It is set during the reign of Henry IV or early Henry V. The play makes no pretense to exist outside contemporary Elizabethan-Era English, middle-class life.

***

In 2001, the year following Katie's sudden demise, my cousin, Madeline Wells, (on the Devine side) and I took a New London Adult and Continuing Education trip to Prague, Czech Republic. It was wonderful. Madeline is the eldest of four siblings, approximately two years younger than I, and slightly shorter. She has always been a most attractive strawberry blonde. She is married to Rikki Wells and they have one beautiful brunette daughter.

Like most cities, Prague has very steep hills, but its center is relatively flat and very walkable with a magnitude of history. I was impressed particularly since our excursion was in August, when most Europeans have gone on vacation. However, at that time, the city, with its hundred church spires, was bustling with activity. Every church held a concert, whether it was chamber music, classical, more modern music, or religious. One might attend a concert at any time of day or at night. Various operas were offered every night of the week. I regret not being able to take advantage of that extensive opera menu, which included Mozart's *The Magic Flute*, Mascagni's *Cavalleria Rusticana*, or Leoncavallo's *Pagliacci.*

I recall vividly a magnificent, medieval astronomical clock that was mounted on the southern wall of the Old Town Hall. It was first installed in 1410, making it the third-oldest astronomical clock in the world ... and the oldest still operating. Obviously, I have a passion for all kinds of clocks and am mesmerized by the intricacies of these ancient time pieces: especially this one that had survived the weather elements over all those years. This particular gem has three main components: the astronomical dial that represents the position of the sun and the moon in the sky, and displaying a variety of astronomical details. Statues of Catholic Saints loom on either side of the clock. "The Walk of the Apostles," revolve hourly around the center while the clock chimes the hour. Other medallion sculptures, notably a figure of a skeleton that represents *Death,* denote the month of the year. Fascinating!

Since Mom's family was a mix of English, Spanish, and French, I decided in 2002 to venture out on my own for a two-week tour of Spain. In booking the tour, I made sure it included *Barcelona.* It was in October, 1771 when, my ancestor, Captain Gabriel Sistare, Sr., sailed all the way across the Atlantic from Barcelona to settle in New London, Connecticut … in the far away land known as America.

While growing up, we always attended the annual Sistare Family Reunions – a tradition. These gatherings were usually held in Southeastern Connecticut at either Fort Shantok in Montville or Rocky Neck State Park in Niantic.

Fort Shantok was the site of the principal Mohegan Tribe settlement between 1636 and 1682. It was originally part of the tribal reservation lands, but the state of Connecticut in the 20th Century took ownership of it, converting it to a state park. In 1995, following legal action by the tribe to recover their native lands, the state returned the park to Mohegan control. In 1993, the grounds were declared a National Historic Landmark: *Fort Shantok Archaeological District*. It is located within the Mohegan Indian Reservation, west of the Thames River and south of the Mohegan Sun casino.

Fort Shantok represents a location of distinction to the Mohegan people, because it is the first site where they settled with Sachem Uncas in the 17th Century. Shantok was used by the Mohegan leader Uncas when fending off attacks from the Narragansetts during 1645. The fort area was used as a burial ground. It contains over a hundred identified graves and is maintained *as Sacred Ground.*

***

Rocky Neck State Park is located on Long Island Sound in the township of Niantic. It is a 710-acre gorgeous popular recreation spot. The public now enjoys all this acreage has to offer, due to farsighted conservationists who secured the land back in 1931. They used personal funds until the State Legislature finally authorized its purchase. Rocky Neck's varied terrain offers the following: camping, picnicking, hiking, saltwater fishing, and, of course, saltwater swimming from its pristine white sand beach and clear waters.

High on the rocky bluffs overlooking Long Island Sound sits an impressive cobblestoned pavilion, marked by stone fireplaces and native wood pillars. Its second floor is available for receptions, private parties, seminars and conferences, seating three-hundred.

Let's return to our Sistare Family gatherings at one of these two local landmarks. My cousin Gertrude was secretary of that organization for twenty-five years. Unfortunately, as older generations passed on, the younger ones failed to keep the family ties together.

Continuing on our two-week tour, the next stop was Barcelona, with its high hills that afford magnificent panoramic views, and miles of level terrain, was another walkable city. Just fascinating. It was of particular interest to me, since it marks the origin of Mom's family settling in Connecticut.

I'll never forget seeing this gargantuan, unfinished cathedral: *Temple Expiatori de la Sagrada Familia*. It was created by architect Antoni Gaudi. His striving for originality was with symbolism inspired by nature. For example: a winged bull represents Saint Luke; a winged man denotes Saint Matthew; an eagle connotes Saint John; and a winged lion signifies Saint Mark. The lower spires are surmounted by communion hosts with sheaves of wheat and chalices with bunches of grapes which represent the Eucharist. The façade faces the rising sun to the northeast, a symbol of Christ's birth. It is divided into three porticos, each of which represents a theological virtue: Hope, Faith, and Charity. The masterpiece became his life's work and simply cannot be missed! It is a UNESCO World Heritage Site.

On November 7, 2010, Pope Benedict XVI consecrated and proclaimed this cathedral a minor basilica. In fact, the Cathedral of the Holy Cross and Saint Eulalia *is* the cathedral of the Archdiocese of Barcelona.

The Sagrada Familia Basilica is recognized as Europe's most unconventional church -- an emblem of a city that likes to think itself as individualistic. The day we were there, as we walked into that glorious cathedral, we heard a soprano soloist singing in Catalan: "Safe in the Hand of God." We recognized immediately the piece as "Amazing Grace." The acoustics carried her glorious voice, which brought tears to our eyes, sent chills up our spines, and Goosebumps all over our arms.

Sculptor Antoni Gaudi (1852-1926) was a Catalan (Spanish) architect known as the greatest exponent of Catalan Modernism. His works are highly individualized, one-of-a-kind style. Most of his works can be found in Barcelona. He considered every detail of his creations and integrated into his architecture such crafts as ceramics, stained glass, wrought ironwork forging, and carpentry. He also introduced new techniques in the treatment of materials, creating *trencadis* which combined waste ceramic pieces.

That magnificent cathedral was unfinished at Gaudi's untimely death, a victim of being hit by a trolley car in Barcelona. He is also buried in the crypt within.

Anticipation is geared to the cathedral's final completion date of June 10, 2026, which will coincide with the 100th anniversary of Gaudi's passing. Upon completion of the spires, the Sagrada Familia will be the tallest church building in the world.

***

Our tour travelled all over Spain from Madrid to Barcelona and to the southern part, including Granada. You will recall when I described the DVD consisting of two movies covering the life and work of Spanish Guitarist Andre Segovia: the second film on that disc was his playing magnificently a wide variety of pieces in the great halls of the Palaces of Alhambra. The Alhambra dates back to the Middle Ages. The stonework is not only breathtaking; but it has been gloriously and meticulously maintained.

While in southern Spain, we actually had the opportunity to cross into Gibraltar, a peninsular on the south-central coast of Spain. It is actually in the Strait of Gibraltar, which connects the Mediterranean and the Atlantic Ocean between Spain and North Africa. There, we saw not only the huge famous *Rock of Gibraltar,* but were enthralled with all of the wild Barbary monkeys ... delightful. Did you know that those monkeys love chocolate? But then ... who doesn't?

Those Barbary monkeys are the only wild primates of their kind on the European continent. My souvenir from that trip was a

Swarovski crystal monkey, standing on its hind legs, a bunch of bananas flung over one shoulder. Just now remembering that glistening monkey brings a smile to my face, as I think about our firsthand experience with all of them.

This tour did include a brief visit to Pamplona. Fortunately for us, it was not the time for the running of the bulls. That to me would have been way too scary and too dangerous!

We went on to visit Seville, where we enjoyed a Flamenco Show, which I loved because of the guitars and their lively music. The dancers were exquisite with all of their supple moves. They say the *Flamenco* is the soul of Andalusia, a section of Spain where Andre Segovia settled. The flamenco is considered to be much more than a dance – *it is a forceful, artistic expression of the sorrows and joys of life.* The dancers improvise from basic movements, following only the rhythm of the guitar ... and their own feelings.

The following day we returned to Madrid for our flight home.

On this particular tour there were nine of us who had booked single accommodations. Consequently, there was always someone with whom to do things, or not, however the spirit moved you.

***

My single booking had worked out so well, my next adventure was a two-week Heart of Europe Tour. We started in London, then on to Amsterdam, Netherlands; Cologne, Rothenberg, Munich, Oberammergau, Bavaria, all in Germany; Innsbruck, Austria; Lucerne, Switzerland; and finally ended the tour in Paris, France.

Our one free day in Paris just happened to be a Tuesday, when the famous Le Louvre Museum was closed. We could have wandered around Paris on our own, but we opted for a tour of Chateau de Versailles, which was magnificent. In thinking back to that excursion, I remember how it rained every time we were *off* the bus, but the sun was out while we traveled *on* the bus. In fact, that weather cycle didn't change — when we were inside touring the Chateau, there was brilliant sunshine, but the minute we walked out into the marble courtyard to stroll their gorgeous gardens, it poured.

For this particular tour, I had booked a single reservation and, unlike the tour of Spain, I was the only single person there. The rest of the people were couples or a family of five. However, they were all friendly, and there was only one time that became *scary* for me. It was in Munich, Germany, when the tour director, following our morning excursion, dropped us off for lunch at Marienplatz, a huge plaza. At the end of that plaza was a Beer Garden, which was comprised of numerous kiosks where you could buy beer, wine, sandwiches, and even soft drinks.

By the time I had pulled together my lunch of a ham and cheese sandwich on a croissant and Coca Cola Light, I had got myself totally turned around and disoriented. I'd lost track of where to go to get back to the Marienplatz, where we would meet the bus. Of course, we were in Germany, where most people spoke … German. I did not. But all was not lost. As I was telling myself not to panic, and assuring myself I could communicate the plaza's name, I heard an *angel's voice:* "Hi, Millie!"

I turned around and there was one of the tour members, sitting and relaxing, and having a beer – *Thank God!* We chatted. I explained my plight, and he very calmly directed me back to Marienplatz. What a relief it was – I'm convinced he was *Heaven Sent* and the only one from our tour group that I saw in the Beer Garden.

***

In the fall of 2003, I decided to see some more of our own country and visited with friends. You remember my telling you about Bill Kelley (scientist, tennis and ski instructor, microscope builder ...) and his wonderful wife, Lois. They had moved from Quaker Hill to Salt Lake City; then to Cottonwood, Arizona, which is a neighbor of Sedona. We took a day trip to the Grand Canyon. There is only one word that describes its magnificence and that word is *awesome. Goose-bump* awesome! In its presence my reaction was aesthetic arrest -- meaning my ordinary life was interrupted, halted for a time while I attempted to take it all in and, contemplate the true magnificence of its vastness.

***

In September, 2004 I took a Holland America Cruise from Seward, Alaska down the coast to Vancouver, British Columbia. It too was breathtaking. I just loved seeing a momma bear and her babies playing in the water on the coast. There is so much to see in our own country and throughout the world. It's all there. I encourage everyone to travel, if at all possible.

The highlight of that tour for me was the helicopter ride over the ice-capped terrain and landing on the glaciers, getting off the plane, and walking around on the them. We were wearing special boots, provided by the flight company, with tread to accommodate walking on those icy behemoths. Of course, we had to be very careful to watch where we were stepping so as not to slip accidentally into a crevasse. In fact, the pilot had warned us to look behind us before backing up to take that special photo ... carelessness and slipping into one of those crevasses could mean disaster. We were indeed fortunate; and everyone heeded those grim warnings. It was a bright sunny spectacular day and there were no mishaps!

Just cruising down the coast of Alaska, the ship would pause, at an angle itself, so we all might catch glimpses of the glaciers cracking, breaking off, and dropping into the ocean with a huge splash. What a thundering sound they made and with such beauty. The contrasts between the glistening white ice and the turquoise water were breathtaking.

***

In 2005 I travelled to Portugal with New London Adult and Continuing Education. We stayed the week near Lisbon in the coastal town of Estoril. We ventured out on day trips from there, including the city of Fatima.

You may be interested to know that Fatima is one of the most famous Marian shrines in the world. Approximately four million people visit it each year. Fatima is a Catholic Title of the Blessed Virgin Mary based on the Marian apparitions of the Virgin Mary reportedly seen by three local shepherd children, between May and October, 1917. The three children were Lucia dos Santos and her cousins Francisco and Jacinta Marto. These sightings were declared worthy of belief on October 13, 1930 by Bishop Jose Alves Correia da Silva.

I believe the members of our entire tour group found their taste buds satisfied when we found this fabulous bakery with all kinds of luscious desserts. There was a small delicate pastry filled with a decadent vanilla cream that oozed out as you ate it. It could be messy and gooey to eat, but … finger-licking good. Oh, so worth it! They came eight in a slim plastic cylinder. Several of us would try to buy a single package and share it with all of our travelling companions. However, our willpower was weakened after the very first bite. We tried to be good but, many of us, upon our return trips from daytime excursions, made a mad dash to that bakery for those delicacies. What a special treat! I've never been able to find anything that even began to resemble that scrumptious little delicacy.

***

A couple years later I did a National Park Tour, which started in Salt Lake City, Utah. It took us to Jackson Hole, Wyoming, which is the beginning of the Grand Tetons – truly gorgeous. We continued up to Yellowstone and saw Old Faithful erupt several times. This trip included the most northern part of Yellowstone – Mammoth Hot Springs – so different and spectacular. One simply must travel and explore in order to get a taste of Mother Nature's magnificence.

As we traveled by bus, we saw all kinds of wildlife: a couple of really big stags with their full antlers, pronghorn antelope, elk, moose (including a mother and her baby), a mother grizzly bear with her two adorable cubs, deer, bison, and the list goes on.

We ended that trip visiting the Black Hills in Keystone, South Dakota. We've all heard of Mount Rushmore, which includes the grandeur of those 60-foot sculpted heads of Presidents George Washington (1732-1799), Thomas Jefferson (1743-1826), Theodore Roosevelt (1858-1919), and Abraham Lincoln (1809-1865). These four presidents were chosen to represent the nation's stunning birth, growth, development, and preservation.

The impact of those sculptures was not lost on me, nor the beauty of that national park and its focal presentation of presidential memorials. However, I was most moved by visiting the nearby Crazy Horse Memorial that was still under construction. This sculpture memorializes a fiercely independent Lakota Sioux warrior and eventually it will include his loyal horse as well.

***

Sculptor Korczak Ziolkovski began the world's largest mountain carving in 1948. Members of his family and their supporters are continuing his artistic intent to create a massive

335

statue; it will be 641 feet long and 563 feet high. (For comparison, an American football field is 360 feet long and 160 feet wide.) In 1998 workers completed the carving of Crazy Horse's face, a mere 87 1/2-feet-tall that looms over the Black Hills he had ruled. It is approximately thirty-feet taller than our presidents' memorials on Mount Rushmore. They continue to work on thinning the remaining mountain to form a 219-foot-high horse's head.

Crazy Horse was born in the Black Hills of South Dakota in 1841. He was the son of the Oglala Sioux shaman, also named Crazy Horse. Boys were traditionally not named until they had had an experience that earned them one. As a child, Crazy Horse, The Younger, was called "Curly Hair" and was also known as "Light-Haired Boy." Those names attributed to his naturally curly blonde hair. As an adolescent, Crazy Horse earned the name "His Horse Looking" – but was more commonly known as "Curly." In 1858, following a battle with Arapaho warriors, he was given his father's name of Crazy Horse. His father then took the name "Worm."

Crazy Horse's father was a medicine man in the tribe. He took in many people from all over, because he had had the confidence that he could *cure* them. The name Worm likely comes from the *wood worm,* which is capable of eating through hard wood, and is also considered a powerful medicine animal.

This younger warrior participated in numerous battles on behalf of his people, struggling to secure their native lands for the tribes. He was not one to follow his tribe's usual customs. He shrugged off many of the Sioux traditions and rituals. In fact, in 1854, he purposefully ignored those required rituals; instead, he rode off into the prairies for a *vision quest.* After fasting for two days, he had a paranormal encounter with an unadorned horseman who instructed him to present himself in the same way … no more than one feather, and never a war bonnet. The visionary horseman he beheld also told him to toss dust over his horse before entering battle; he was also told to place a stone behind his ear, and to never take anything from the Sacred Grounds for himself.

337

These instructions were carried out by Crazy Horse throughout the remainder of his life. In one case, Crazy Horse pulled soldiers out of disputed forts that were under General William Tecumseh Sherman's command. This was after a treaty had been signed that *gave the native population ownership of the Black Hills in South Dakota.* He also came up against General George Custer's encroachment into the Black Hills, while he and others were searching for gold; *thus, violating the treaties with the Indian tribes.* This also ushered in civilian miners who vastly outnumbered the Native population. In the Battle of Little Big Horn, Crazy Horse led one thousand warriors to outflank Custer's forces and help seal the general's crushing defeat and eventual death.

This historic encounter became known as *Custer's Last Stand.*

Crazy Horse died in 1877 at the age of *thirty-five,* after attempting to negotiate with the military; but he was betrayed, once again, by the duplicity of unscrupulous officers during a very harsh winter. The young Sioux succumbed in prison after a sadistic soldier shoved a bayonet into his abdomen, piercing his kidneys. Crazy Horse is remembered for his courage, his leadership, and his strength of spirit in the face of near-impossible odds.

I was so taken by the history of this fearless warrior, coupled with the magnificence of his giant eighty-seven-and-a-half-foot sculpture. I was moved to tears. In addition, we were told that at no time during the creation of this masterpiece of tribute, would the people accept any money from the federal government. It was *all* being funded through private donations.

I think back to what we were told about the atrocities committed against our Native Americans, and the devastating impact it had on them. Our inhumanity to fellow human beings is unfathomable! I shake my head tearfully in disbelief.

America's ghosts haunt us ... forever.

***

By now I was becoming known as ... *"Globe-Trotting Millie."*

In 2008 my cousin Grace and I took a Globus Northern European Tour, which included visits to Copenhagen, Denmark; Oslo, Norway; Stockholm, Sweden; St. Petersburg, Russia; and Helsinki, Finland. It is just so exciting to meet the native people in all of these various countries and to learn about their history and culture. We had wonderful tour guides in each of the cities. In fact, as we entered St. Petersburg, Russia, the city-tour guide boarded our bus and stayed with us until we departed that magnificent city.

When we visited the Hermitage Museum -- also known as Catherine's Palace – and were getting off the bus, there was a three-piece brass band that greeted us by playing the Star-Spangled Banner and the Battle Hymn of the Republic. We were deeply touched by that, especially being in Russia ... so far away from home.

The Hermitage Museum is a treasure trove of history and beauty with its exquisite furnishings. Our tour guide showed us gold decorated walls and ceilings, murals, paintings, and chandeliers. We also saw the amber ornately decorated room. The final room had huge, gorgeous paintings by celebrated artists: Rembrandt, Leonardo da Vinci, the French impressionists.

It was all beautiful ... but for my cousin and me, the most memorable was the Russian Ballet *Swan Lake* ... truly magnificent! The exquisite dancers displayed graceful moves and leaps, as if floating on air, and the feelings emanating from those performers was one of glorious, breath-taking perfection. St. Petersburg, of course, is known as *The Cradle of the Ballet.*

***

The next year my cousin and I took a Globus Celtic Highlights Tour, which was a fast-paced trip and covered Scotland, England, Wales, Ireland, and Northern Ireland. It was in this visit that I noticed the thatched roofs had been replaced with traditional roofs, except on historic buildings.

***

In 2011, I enjoyed touring the Canadian Rockies. We were bussed from Vancouver, British Columbia to Banff and Lake Louise via the northern route. Our return trip was mostly onboard the Rocky Mountaineer Train along the southern route. Unfortunately, that wonderful excursion was interrupted by a *freight train derailment on the tracks*. Consequently, we had to wait for hours, the arrival of busses to take us from just outside of Banff, and then to Kamloops where they put us up for the night. Imagine the number of busses needed to handle all of that train's passengers! To boot, some of those old busses were pretty rickety: unusable bathrooms, brakes that were suspect, and a number of other malfunctions; but they did finally get us safely to Kamloops and ultimately to our hotel.

The next morning, we were once again able to reboard the Rocky Mountaineer and completed our trip. Again, the highlight of that trip for me was the helicopter ride on a crystal-clear, bright sunny day, soaring over the snow-capped Canadian Rockies. It was so exciting flying among the mountain peaks and valleys – lots of "oooos" and "aahhhs" -- truly magnificent and utterly breathtaking!

***

In my many adventures, I was also able to take a wonderful Viking Cruise in 2014. I flew from Boston to Geneva, Switzerland, having to change planes in Paris at De Gaulle Airport. The hotel was overlooking Lake Geneva, with the glorious Swiss Alps on one side, and the spectacular French Alps on the other. To me it was a taste of what Heaven must be like.

From there we were transported to Basel, Switzerland, where we boarded the Viking Cruise Ship. We cruised up the Rhine through Germany to Amsterdam, and then flew home. Along the

343

way, the ship provided tours of various ports and areas, which were all fascinating and most enjoyable. One in particular was in Schoenwald, Germany nestled deep in the Black Forest. It was in 1737 when it became known as the origin of the infamous *cuckoo clock*. We watched the making of those intricately designed carvings by the hands of masterful craftsmen. Each one, different in size and with unique little chalets, featured a little cuckoo bird popping out of the upper window, always right on the hour.

While we visited the home of the cuckoo clocks, the village bakers showed us how to make the rich, decadent German Chocolate Cake. It is a rich cake, hand-frosted with coconut icing, and contains chopped pecans that filled the two-layers, and the outside of it as well. This luscious delicacy is topped with a chocolate ganache drizzled over it. *Yummy!*

***

While traveling the Romantic Middle Rhine, where the river winds past quaint villages and medieval castles, the cruise director provided an orated history of those mighty fortifications. This particular section of the Rhine provides a window into the past with unmatched vistas. It has castles on either side of it. One is the Medieval Marksburg Castle, built in the 13th Century, that was chiseled into the slate bedrock of a mountain peak. Consequently, due to its strong fortification, it is recognized as one of Germany's more formidable castles. *It has never been besieged by enemies.* It is still filled with a wide variety of knights' swords, lances, helmets, and full outfits of armor.

I must say, the tour guide had warned us of demanding physical activities, which included extensive hiking, riding, and high altitudes. She had also forewarned us that hardy walking could be difficult due to unpaved surfaces, multiple stairs and steep inclines, including cobblestones. I noticed a couple of people from our group had walking sticks for this adventure, which I discovered would have been a great help. I wished I'd thought to bring one with me. However, I discovered that chivalry is still alive and well, as at one point I began to slip on loose gravel mixed among the cobblestones. Fortunately, for me there were two stalwart gentlemen who came to my rescue by extending their arms and saving me from falling. I was most grateful to that gallant duo.

On this glorious adventure, I once again met fascinating people from many different countries and from all walks of life. I highly recommend the smaller cruise ships, which provide much more intimacy with fellow passengers, rather than the huge ones that have become cities unto themselves.

Chapter 13

Trip of a Lifetime

Prior to that Ontario, Canada and Niagara Falls trip with my sister Katie, the regional branch manager for our bank had been serving on the board of the Eugene O'Neill Theater. He had one raffle ticket left for a mere fifty dollars. He, of course, was a good salesman: "Millie, this ticket is the winning one and has your name on it!" He exclaimed. "Just imagine, you and your sister aboard the elegant Venice-Simplon Orient Express Train!"

We bank officers always try supporting each other, but *fifty dollars for one ticket?* What was the Orient Express? Well, I broke down and gave him the money, which finished his allotment of tickets to sell just ahead of his having to report at the next board meeting.

I knew the raffle proceeds were benefiting the Eugene O'Neill Theater Center in Waterford, Connecticut, a 501(C)(3) non-profit organization founded in 1964 by George C. White ... a worthy cause. However, all I knew about the Orient Express was that it was a fancy train only the rich and famous toured on. I also knew that Agatha Christie had written a book: *Murder on the Orient Express,* which had been made into a movie with Kenneth Branagh, Penelope Cruz, and William Dafoe.

Let me fill you in on the history of this luxurious train. The Venice-Simplon Orient Express was recreating the route of the first Orient-Express train, which left Paris on October 4, 1883, travelling to Istanbul via Vienna and Budapest. Luxury train travel to Eastern Europe had ceased with the outbreak of the Second World War, but the lifting of the "Iron Curtain" meant, that as of June 13, 1991, passengers could once again travel to Hungary in a resplendent of a by-gone era. This was the fabulous trip that was being offered through the raffle.

Now I'll take a moment to describe the Eugene O'Neill Theater that would benefit from the proceeds of this particular raffle. It is a multi-disciplinary institution that has had a transformative effect on American theater. The O'Neill pioneered play development and stage readings as a tool for new plays and musicals, and is home to the National Theater Institute, established in 1970, an intensive study-away semester for undergraduates. Its major theater conferences include the National Playwrights, the National Critics, the National Musical Theater, and the Cabaret & Performance.

Eugene O'Neill (October 16, 1888 – November 27, 1953) was an American playwright and Nobel Laureate in Literature. His poetically titled plays were among the first to introduce into United States drama techniques of realism that were earlier associated with Russian playwright Anton Chekhov. Such techniques were also utilized by Norwegian playwright, Henrik Ibsen, and Swedish playwright, August Strindberg. The drama *Long Day's Journey into Night* is often numbered on the short list of finest United States plays in the 20th Century.

Eugene was the son of Irish immigrants, actor James O'Neill and Mary Ellen Quinlan. Since his parents traveled a lot, due to being in the theater, Eugene was sent to St. Aloysius Academy for Boys: a Catholic boarding school in the Riverdale section of the Bronx, New York.

The O'Neill family reunited for summers at the Monte Cristo Cottage, overlooking the Thames River in New London, Connecticut. Consequently, the establishment of the Eugene O'Neill Theater in Waterford, Connecticut with all of its great shows. We also have a spectacular 250-pound bronze sculpture, created by Norman Lagasse, of Eugene as a boy of approximately six years old seated, on a rock overlooking the sea, and wearing high-buttoned shoes and an Eton cap. It is located on City Pier near the lighthouse in downtown New London. Yes, this is the statue I often beheld from two of my huge tower office windows. It was dedicated on October 16, 1988, the one hundredth anniversary from O'Neill's birth. It is a *must* see for tourists to this area.

***

Now back to our returning home from that delightful visit to Ontario, Canada. After driving twelve long hours, Katie and I were so glad to be home again. We were relieved knowing we had no immediate plans to travel once again. Although we were tired, but happy, we were ready for a good night's sleep. We felt we had had enough traveling to last us awhile.

As they say with the best laid plans of mice and men, our plans for sleep went astray. About ten o'clock that night the telephone rang. One usually dreads an unexpected call at that hour, or later, which often spells bad news or a wrong number. Today, we usually assume it's a robocall: *Hello, this is John from Creative Travel, and you have won ... blah, blah, blah, (Click).* Consequently, today we carefully check the caller ID before thinking of answering.

However, this was 1990 and so I answered the phone. It was Marilyn Glassman who was chairing the fund-raising committee for the Eugene O'Neill Theater in Waterford. I knew Marilyn as a wonderful long-time, enthusiastic and energetic volunteer, but I thought that she wouldn't be calling me for a donation at such a late hour. Or would she? And she was always very persuasive. She was the wife of Sandy Glassman, a prominent attorney in town, who served on the O'Neill's board. Both were big, long-time supporters of this great organization.

Always vivacious, Marilyn was particularly exuberant as she informed me: "The winning raffle ticket has just been drawn for a trip for two on the Venice-Simplon Orient Express ... *Millie, you are the lucky winner*!"

Unfortunately, I was so tired from having driven for twelve hours, and she was so excited, as usual, I had a hard time absorbing what she was attempting to convey to me. After her repeating the details three times, she asked, "Millie, are you going to be in your office on Monday? If so, I'll bring the brochure to you."

Needless to say, I had forgotten completely about that *raffle* and the date of its drawing, or what it was all about. In my mind, I'd written the price of the ticket off as a contribution, although I was delighted to be the *winner*. The following Monday, Marilyn scurried into my office, brochure in hand, describing the fabulous prize: a trip for two aboard the Orient Express train, details to be worked out with the travel agent. Wow ... that was a spectacular prize! There was only *one little hitch* causing a delay in our being able to book this awesome trip. With the specter of the Persian Gulf War hanging over us, we wouldn't be allowed to go until it was over.

***

We had all studied in school about the many wars that had impacted our country since its beginning. World Wars I and II, as well as the Korean War, were most familiar to us since we had had grandparents, parents, or relatives who had served. Being age three, when the end of World War II was declared in 1945, I remember so well how excited our parents were, and my running out the front door, dancing on the lawn. I also recall having to have shades drawn and knowing where we needed to go in case a bomb was dropped on the United States; such as, our own Naval Submarine Base in Groton. I remember my parents telling us how our Uncle Bill, one of Pop's younger brothers, was lost at sea in 1941, when his submarine was sunk in the Magellan Straits. That shocking news was devastating to Pop's whole family.

Here we were involved in yet another war. And our servicemen, some of who had served in Vietnam, were called back to fight once again. Those of us having graduated high school in 1960 recalled many of our young men graduating and immediately going off to Vietnam to fight a war we couldn't comprehend. We were all scared for them and prayed for the help of the Lord to keep them safe. We also recalled many of those young men being maimed or having died fighting in that undeclared war. I've always felt for those veterans who have been dealing with the horrors of what they had experienced during that terrible era.

Little did we suspect, fifteen years later, we would once again be shipping off to yet another war, our next generation of young men and women. I know my thoughts went to "Here we go again." Obviously, we hadn't learned our lesson from all the previous combats.

As it turned out, the Persian Gulf War, code name *Operation Desert Storm,* was in place August 2, 1990 – February 28, 1991 (also known as the One-hundred-Day War), so we weren't allowed to travel until it ended. It was for operations leading to the buildup of troops in defense of Kuwait. That war was waged by coalition forces from thirty-five nations led by the United States against Iraq in response to its invasion of Kuwait arising supposedly from oil pricing and production disputes.

On August 2nd, the Iraqi Army invaded Kuwait, which was met with international condemnation and brought immediate economic sanctions against Iraq by members of the United Nations Security Council. An array of nations joined the coalition, forming the largest military alliance since World War II.

Of course, the Vietnam War, known as the 10,000 Day War, was the first one to have news media reporting from the sites. The United States was among those doing so. However, the Persian Gulf War marked the introduction of *live* news broadcasts directly from the front lines of battle, principally by the United States' network of CNN. Reporters had to don gas masks!

The initial conflict to expel Iraqi troops from Kuwait began with an aerial and naval bombardment on January 17, 1991, continuing for five weeks. That was followed by a ground assault on February 24. This was a decisive victory for the coalition forces that liberated Kuwait.

***

Back to the spring of 1990 and my winning that magnificent trip on the Venice-Simplon Orient Express Train to which we were looking forward. You will recall that I'd received the exuberant phone call from Marilyn Glassman from the O'Neill. No, she wasn't looking for a contribution to the Eugene O'Neill Theater, but informing me of my very special raffle winnings. In spite of being exhausted from driving twelve long hours from Ontario to home, I did thank her for her call and looked forward to receiving the detailed brochure on the very next Monday at the bank. Once I finished that phone conversation, I attempted to tell Katie about winning the trip. Of course, I couldn't describe the winning trip to her, except to tell her it would be on a train and I'd be getting a brochure with details on Monday at the office. Monday morning came and Marilyn, the fund-raising chair for the Eugene O'Neill Theater, delivered the trip brochure, as promised.

With the details about this luxurious train trip in hand, I was ecstatic! Its value was $7,500 ... and I'd *only paid $50 for the one ticket*. Now, wasn't that a fabulous return on investment! Amazing how certain details can change one's perspective. When I was given the chance to buy that raffle ticket for a mere fifty dollars, the cost seemed high. When I realized the fifty-dollar ticket had grown into this extremely valuable lifetime opportunity, I was thrilled!

My sister Katie and I figured we'd be taking the trip together. While the Persian Gulf War was still on, we talked briefly about the pending trip, but couldn't make actual plans.

By that fall, Katie had decided that she wouldn't attempt to go on the Orient Express trip with me. She was not enamored with train travel due to the rocking motion, and anticipated the quarters would be cramped. With her height she was sure the bed would be too short and too narrow. In addition, she was going through a stressful job search. Consequently, she suggested that I invite my dear friend of about thirty years, Beryl Hobart, to accompany me.

After making sure that Katie really did not want to go on this famous train, I invited Beryl instead.

Beryl and I spoke often long-distance by phone. It was natural for us to talk during the Holidays. She knew Katie, and wasn't surprised to hear that she was reneging on joining me for this fabulous trip. I informed her that Katie had suggested I offer the trip to her, which I was thrilled to do. She was overwhelmed with the invitation, but still needed a little time to talk with her family. Obviously, there was no rush to reply due to the dangers of the ongoing Persian Gulf War. Within a short period of time, Beryl let me know that she would be delighted to go. Her family was thrilled that she was taking advantage of such a spectacular opportunity.

As it turned out, the Persian Gulf War ended rather abruptly with Saddam Hussein's withdrawal from Kuwait. One could hear the world's audible collective sigh of relief. It's over! Normalcy had returned. Amazing!

Of course, the memory of Vietnam was still in people's minds.

As was the beautiful rendition of the song: *From A Distance,* made famous in 1990 by singer and songwriter, Bette Midler, with its meaningful and poignant lyrics:

"From a distance
The world looks blue and green
And the snow-capped mountains white
From a distance
The ocean meets the stream
And the eagle takes to flight.

From a distance
There is harmony
And it echoes through the land.
It's the voice of hope; It's the voice of peace
It's the voice of every man.

From a distance we all have enough
And no one is in need.
And there are no guns, no bombs, and no disease
No hungry mouths to feed.

From a distance we are instruments
Marching in a common band;
Playing songs of hope, playing songs of peace.
They're the songs of every man.
God is watching us. God is watching us.
God is watching us from a distance.

From a distance you look like my friend
Even though we are at war.
From a distance I just cannot comprehend
What all this fighting is for.

From a distance there is harmony
And it echoes through the land.
And it's the hope of hopes, it's the love of loves,
It's the heart of every man.

It's the hope of hopes, it's the love of loves,
This is the song of every man;
And God is watching us, God is watching us from a distance.
Oh, God is watching us. God is watching;
God is watching us from a distance."

***

Beryl and I were able finally to go on this fabulous trip in June, 1991. Her husband and family drove her from Biddeford, Maine down to Logan Airport in Boston, Massachusetts. I took the train up to Boston from New London. We met there. We were both 'over the moon' about that pending trip. Our respective families were truly excited for us.

Both of us were so looking forward to the overnight flight to London, England. We had each done a good amount of flying on jets, props, and piper cubs, and enjoyed the feeling of flying, which we loved. In fact, Beryl was so enamored with flying that she had wanted to become a stewardess. However, with her mother being a highly regarded nurse and her father, an engineer, they did not think being a stewardess was an appropriate career choice for her. Consequently, Beryl listened to her dear parents and followed their guidance by becoming a highly needed medical lab technician.

We were ecstatic to finally land at Heathrow Airport about six in the morning, where we'd start our exciting journey. We may have dozed on the plane, but far too excited to sleep. It was thrilling to see the name *Devine* in bold print held up by the handsome, charming, middle-aged chauffeur who would help us with our luggage, and take us to the Hampton Hotel for our two-night stay, which was a stone's throw from London's Theater District. Upon arrival at the hotel, we were immediately served hot

English Breakfast Tea and shortly thereafter shown to our elegant room, approximately seven o'clock that morning.

We decided, since it was our first trip to London, we would utilize our free day by touring that great city, which we did. We had heard so much about London pubs (Katie and I had enjoyed them in Ireland), that we went looking for one during lunch. We were not disappointed. We knew we'd be having our main meal at the hotel that evening. So, we ordered a light lunch of egg and tuna salad croissant sandwiches, served with lettuce and tomato, along with our diet cokes.

That afternoon we visited the Changing of the Guards at Buckingham Palace, toured the glorious Westminster Abbey, went to the Tower of London where we saw the fabulous crowned jewels. Those jewels are the world's best-known collection of gorgeous queen's crowns, as well as Princess Diana's tiaras, plus scepters, orbs, and swords used at coronations. What a dazzling exhibition of jeweled objects!

The tour guide was excellent and pointed out Piccadilly Square, Kensington Palace and Gardens, Hyde Park, Victoria and Albert Museum ... and that famous iconic clock, Big Ben. As we traveled around that glorious city, filled with so much history, we passed Parliament as well. We only hit the highlights in that particular day's visit to London. We knew we'd have to plan another trip to take in more of its breathtaking wonders.

We definitely were ready to sleep that night. In fact, Beryl told me the next morning that I fell asleep actually in mid-sentence of whatever I was talking about. Of course, when I awoke, I had no idea what I had been saying. Poor Beryl never knew what I was attempting to share with her. We chuckle as that mystery lives on to this day.

After a good night's sleep, the next day we took a morning tour. We realized that here we were, after the Persian Gulf War, finally in London and that night, with the concierge's assistance, we were going to the theater to see *Dancing at Lughnasa*. This was a 1990 play written by dramatist Brian Friel. It was set in County

Donegal in Ulster in the north of Ireland in August, 1936 in the fictional town of Ballybeg. It is a memory play told from the point of view of the adult Michael Evans, the narrator. He recounts the summer in his aunts' cottage back when he was seven years old. It was very well presented and lent insights to the audience of the poverty experienced by so many people during the 1930s.

Long after our return home, we were fascinated when that play came to Broadway in New York. We followed all of the fascinating hype from the media before it even arrived … and later on from its rave reviews. Great fun for us.

The morning after the performance, our same debonair chauffeur picked us up once again at our hotel and drove us to the railroad station. We were so excited to actually be going on the Venice Simplon-Orient-Express Train's inaugural run. It left from Platform 2 of London's famous Victoria Station, to Budapest, Hungary via Paris, Salzburg, and Vienna.

Sending that special train on its inaugural journey, a Hungarian gypsy band with violins, guitar, and cimbalom entertained passengers before boarding the British Pullman day-train that would take us through the picturesque countryside down to Folkstone, in Kent at the base of the White Cliffs of Dover. On that special day, June 13, 1991, we were greeted by four of the train's employees (who normally work in Reservations and Marketing) wearing traditional Hungarian peasant costumes of embroidered waistcoat, white blouse, and colorful-circular skirt. These four women were serving excellent Hungarian Tokai wine to all of us passengers. All of the flowers in the VSOE check-in lounge and on the Pullman were red, white, and green: the colors of the national flag of Hungary.

I had never seen, nor to my knowledge, heard of a cimbalom, which is a type of chordophone composed of a large trapezoidal box with metal strings stretched across its top. It is a musical instrument commonly found in the group of Central Eastern European nations and cultures, not only Hungary, but also

Slovakia, Czech Republic, Croatia, Romania, Ukraine, and Poland. It is a fascinating instrument to hear, as well as to watch the talented musician playing it.

This pullman carriage would take us to the base of the magnificent White Cliffs of Dover, from where we would transfer from the train to the ferry in order to cross the English Channel. While awaiting the boarding of the ferry, we could see and hear the cooing doves nesting in those rugged, steep cliffs. We could also see the channel's tempestuous white caps and knew its reputation for *choppy and rough crossings.*

The English Channel lived up to its reputation. Our crossing was particularly rough. So much so, that many of us were sick. When we boarded that ferry, we Venice-Simplon Orient Express passengers were ushered into a lounge. They were not only selling drinks, but passing rich-fried hors d'oeuvres. The air was full of that pungent greasy smell from their frying. My stomach was beginning to feel queasy. I turned to Beryl, and suggested we might do better out on deck in the fresh air instead.

Wouldn't you know it, just as we got settled on a bench on deck, a man smoking a cigar, strolled right by us. That's all it took. I began retching, along with numerous other passengers.

I cannot imagine anyone desiring to *swim* across that English Channel. However, there have been many brave souls ... men and women. The first woman to do so was an American, Gertrude Ederle. *She beat the men's record by two hours on August 6, 1926,* swimming the thirty-five miles in fourteen-and-a-half hours. During her swim, she battled rapidly changing tides, six-foot waves, frigid temperatures, and those ugly stinging jellyfish. She was known as the *Queen of Waves*. God bless her!

By the time Gertrude Ederle succeeded in this feat, she was already an Olympic Medalist and world record holder. She held that esteemed record until 1950, when Florence Chadwick, also American, completed the crossing from France to England in thirteen hours and twenty minutes.

After that rough ferry crossing of the English Channel, we Orient Express passengers were relieved to be standing on firm ground once again (*"Terra Firma!"* we sighed in delight); ready to board the magnificent navy and gold-colored carriages, which made up the VSOE's Continental Train. The two-day, one-night journey for us to Vienna was truly elegant. We were serenaded in the lounge-car with Hungarian music, and the gourmet meals served so elegantly in the dining car which also followed the Hungarian theme.

Because it was the inaugural trip to Budapest, Prince and Princess Michael of Kent, England were also on board. Their cabin just happened to be at the opposite end of the carriage car from ours. Whenever the train stopped in a station, we would all emerge from our cabins and visit in the corridor, or outside on the platform. These were gracious and charming people ... a positively stunning couple.

There were two possible seating times for dinner while on the train – 6:00 P.M. or 8:00 P.M. Beryl and I had been assigned the

6:00 P.M. which was fine for us; we were early eaters even back then.

The food presentations were works of art! The meal of baked salmon was delicious and the dessert – I just had to take a picture. It was so colorful with its three differently sculpted and colored mousses. One was light orange, another was white, and the third was more of an olive green ... such delicate taste and so scrumptious!

We were particularly impressed by the quantity of silverware at each place setting. As we sat down, and looking it all over, we said, "Mom taught me to start from the outside and work towards the plate. But I don't recall her ever talking about the silverware at the head of our plates." Obviously, when it was time to use the latter silverware, the waiter came and placed it where it belonged on either side of our plates. Consequently, we neither embarrassed ourselves nor anyone else.

All passengers had been encouraged to dress for the period of the 1920s. Beryl and I being conservative New Englanders had discussed this before leaving home. We were conscious of how much baggage we'd be taking, especially in confined cabin quarters. We had opted to keep it simple by wearing black with pearls; we figured we'd be just fine.

However, there were imaginative, flamboyant couples who went all out with their 1920s attire. They looked like they were already to do the Charleston, the ladies wearing their short skirts with tassels and tight-fitting hats, with only a little hair showing around their edges.

While some of the passengers were strutting around like peacocks, there was one particularly outstanding couple seated near us who looked absolutely stunning. This handsome gentleman, with his broad smile, wore a black tuxedo and a bright red bowtie, and matching cummerbund. His stunning wife had a beautifully sculpted body and wore a gorgeous bright red sheath gown, with three-quarter length black gloves, and a black dinner hat. Yes, her red gown matched his bowtie and cummerbund. They were smashingly elegant and charming to boot.

This divine dinner was not only stylish and refined; but we were actually eating while this notorious Orient Express Train was stopped at the station in Paris, France. We were so excited to think we were actually having dinner in the fabulous, historic, and cultural city of Paris! Unfortunately, it was dusk so it was difficult to see much of that great city; but it was fun just knowing that's where we were having our dinner. We decided to add Paris and the French countryside to our list of places we needed to explore another time.

Following dinner, we were escorted into the previous railroad carriage – the cocktail lounge with its magnificent grand piano. We had a chance to relax and enjoy the wonderful variety of music. There was something to satisfy everyone's musical taste, including a long list of Broadway show theme songs, such as *Sound of Music*, (My mind went right to the opening of that movie with Julie Andrews singing its theme song and dancing on the mountain tops in Austria "The Hills are Alive with the Sound of Music". It registered with us that here we were on our way to Austria and would be seeing all of that).

When they played *West Side Story*, we immediately recognized "There's a Place for Us", which took us back to the year Beryl and I had met in Boston. They also played excerpts from *Oklahoma*, and from *Phantom of the Opera*. The music was wonderful! How much better does it get?

During dinner, our cabin had transformed from daytime into nighttime. Our sofa had been converted to a single bed and an overhead bunk bed had also been prepared. Since Beryl is averse to heights, she took the lower berth; I climbed the ladder to the upper one. Eventually Beryl and I decided to turn in for the night. We were just too excited about all we were experiencing. We just couldn't sleep. Around midnight we decided to get up and write postcards. That way, the cards could be mailed first thing in the morning from the train. Once those were done, we did manage to get a little sleep, due to the rocking motion of the train.

While we were attempting to sleep, the train traveled through tunnels and every so often you could see its lights reflecting off the limestone of the Dolomite Mountains located in northeastern Italy. They form a part of the Southern Limestone Alps and extend from the River Adige in the west to the Piave Valley in the east.

We had had the option of taking the train all the way to Budapest; but since neither of us had ever been to Vienna, we opted to make that our destination. There again, we were met by a pleasant, handsome, young red-haired chauffeur. What a heart-throb. In our estimation, he should have been in the movies and he was a true gentleman. He helped us with our bags, and drove us to the Sacher Hotel.

This five-star, luxurious, historic hotel was once the rendezvous for high society. It has remained the cultural cornerstone throughout its illustrious history.

The focal point of the majority of guest rooms were the magnificent Maria Theresa Imperial Cut-Crystal Chandeliers …

breathtaking! While we were out for dinner, our room was prepared by the maid, who had placed a house special delicacy on each of our pillows ... a *Sacher Torte*. It was truly a decadent work of art with all of its layers: semi-sweet chocolate, apricot preserves, dark rum-flavored cake. We agreed it was scrumptious; but we could never attempt to recreate such a flavorful masterpiece.

This gorgeous historic hotel was just across the street from the Vienna State Opera House. The New Year's Eve concerts are broadcast annually via public television; they can be seen on television here in the states, and likely throughout the world ... all emanating from this magnificent concert hall.

This famous hotel is also a very short walk from where the Spanish Riding School of Vienna is situated. The facility is the show place where the gorgeous, sleek white Lipizzaner Stallions demonstrate their *haute ecole* -- high school moments of classical dressage. (The guiding of a horse through a series of complex maneuvers by slight movements of the rider's hands, legs and weight.) The dressage includes the highly controlled, stylized jumps, and other subtle movements known as the *"airs above the ground."* We enjoyed thoroughly their gracefully, choreographed, high-stepping, precision performance!

The Lipizzaner is a breed of horse originally from Lipica in Slovenia. The Lipica stud farm was established in 1580 and is the world's oldest continuously operating stud farm.

The breed has been endangered numerous times by warfare that swept Europe, including the War of the First Coalition: World Wars I and II. The rescue of the Lipizzaner horses during World War II by American troops was made famous by the Disney movie: *Miracle of the White Stallions.*

All of those magnificent opportunities were located, within walking distance of our hotel, but also at Stephansdom Plaza, home of St. Stephen's 13th Century cathedral; commonly known by its German title as St. Stephan's. A cathedral has stood on that site for over 800 years! It is the mother church of the Roman Catholic Archdiocese of Vienna and the seat of its Archbishop.

This Romanesque and Gothic form of the cathedral today was built following World War II, during which it had sadly been reduced to rubble.

Reconstruction began immediately after the war, with a limited reopening December 12, 1948 and a full reopening April 23, 1952. It is built of limestone. The cathedral measures 351 feet long, 130 feet wide, and 446 feet at its highest point. In 1991 when we were there, we could see that soot and other forms of air pollution over the decades had accumulated on its exterior, giving it a black color. When my cousin Grace and I visited St. Stephan's much more recently, it was covered in scaffolding and was being returned to its glistening original white.

***

Returning to 1991 and Beryl's and my strolling that plaza, we entered the cathedral's main doors and were greeted with the glorious organ playing while accompanying a soloist. Her crystal-clear high, expressive soprano voice filled the cathedral with resounding music … oh, how those perfect high notes, breathtakingly pure, sent chills down Beryl's and my spines and tears to our eyes.

After that fabulous visit to the cathedral, Beryl and I continued strolling through the plaza. Our musical love was caressed once again by a talented young woman playing the classical guitar. The piece she played was the memorable *Songs My Mother Taught Me,* written by the famous Czech composer Antonin Leopold Dvorak (1841-1904). We stood there, mesmerized by the absolute splendor of her playing while she serenaded all of us. The beauty of her musicality ... breathtaking! We felt as if she were playing just for us. *It was that special.*

No doubt, you've had similar experiences in your travels of talented musicians serenading the public on street corners or in parks, such as Central Park in New York City. Perhaps you've been not only drawn into listening to beautiful music, but joining in and singing as well.

We also dropped some cash in her opened case. Young artists need all the help and encouragement possible. It was wonderful, especially to me since I was studying classical guitar at the time.

Most everyone is familiar with electric guitars and their steel strings. Musicians, such as the famous Jimi Hendrix (1942-1970), wear picks on their fingers to attack those steel strings. Classical guitarists, wear no picks, but do all of their playing on nylon or gut strings by finger-picking.

We have the great Spanish guitarist, Andre Segovia (1893-1987), to thank for transcribing and adapting these classical or baroque masterpieces of Chopin, Mozart, and Bach for classical guitar and for promoting them. In addition, he enhanced the works of classical guitarists, Fernando Sor and Francisco Tarrega.

Fernando Sor (1778-1839), a Spanish classical guitarist and composer, was known as the Beethoven of that beautiful instrument. His contemporaries considered him to be the best guitarist in the world.

Francisco Tarrega, (1852-1909), another Spanish classical guitarist from the Romantic Period, is known for such pieces as *Recuerdos de la Alhambra*, and is often called, "the Father of Classical Guitar." He is considered one of the greatest guitarists of all time.

Prior to Segovia's musical adaptations, the classical guitar was only heard in bars and on street corners. There was no studying classical guitar in music conservatories in those days. It was just too quiet of an instrument for concert halls. Segovia wrote and transcribed all kinds of music for it and played it to sold-out audiences over his lifetime in concert halls throughout the world.

As a child he studied piano and cello, but his interest could not be diverted from the guitar. There were no teachers of the classical guitar, so Segovia taught himself, basing his own techniques on his own intuitions. He gave his first concert in 1909 while a student at the Granada Musical Institute. By 1916 he was performing in Barcelona, and later in Madrid. From 1919 to 1923 he toured South America. He first performed in Paris in 1924. By that time, he had developed an international reputation. His first American tour was arranged by Fritz Kreisler, the Viennese violinist – who played the guitar on his own privately – persuaded Francis Charles Coppicus from the Metropolitan Musical Bureau to present the guitarist in New York.

While Segovia was hop-scotching around the world over his seventy-eight-year career, Katie and I were blessed to see and hear him (age 93) play at Jorgensen Center for the Performing Arts, located on our own University of Connecticut's campus in Storrs, Connecticut. What a thrill that was for me! Imagine at age 93, still playing flawlessly that wonderful, gentle, mellow instrument. Music was part of his soul and reached the packed auditorium that night, which seats twenty-six hundred. He played masterpieces from Chopin, Bach, Mozart, Sor, and Tarrega, while also sharing much lighter music, such as *Malaguena,* which is more of a flamenco style piece.

Segovia's biography is absolutely fascinating. In 1958 he received the Grammy Award for Best Classical Performances,

Instrumentalist for recording *Segovia Golden Jubilee.* Two very different films were made of his life and work – one he did at age 75 titled: *Segovia at Los Olivos,* from his home on the Costa del Sol; the other when he was 84, *The Song of the Guitar,* which was filmed at the glorious Palaces of Alhambra in Granada. Both of those films are included in a single DVD available under the title, *Andres Segovia In Portrait.* The large open area with the narrow pool was in the Comares Palace's exquisite *Courtyard of the Myrtles.* The other outstanding scene in that movie was when he was playing in the *Courtyard of the Lions.*

***

From Vienna, Beryl's and my first-class trip back-tracked to Salzburg via the Euro-rail. We had chosen to be there during the special 1991 Mozart Anniversary Music Festival of opera, classical music concerts, and theater. It was the two hundredth anniversary since Mozart's passing. As it turned out, we were staying in a gorgeous, ancient, five-star Goldener-Hirsch Hotel, which had hosted the rich and famous: Julie Andrews, Richard Burton, Clark

Gable, Placido Domingo, Douglas Fairbanks, Ingrid Bergman, and many more. This glorious old hotel, with its uneven floors, indicating many additions to it over the years, was in the heart of the old town of Salzburg on a quaint, narrow pedestrian lane, and within a short walk to Mozart's home and birthplace.

Wolfgang Amadeus Mozart was born on January 27, 1756 in Salzburg. At the time of his birth, Salzburg was the capital of the *Archbishopric*, an ecclesiastical principality in what is now Austria.

Mozart was a prolific and influential composer of the Classical Period. He wrote more than six hundred works: symphonies, concertos, chamber, operatic, and choral music. Portions of his *Requiem* were largely unfinished at the time of his early death at age thirty-five. He is considered one of the greatest classical composers of all time.

We obtained, through the concierge, tickets to a wonderful Mozart concert in Mirabelle Palace, where the movie, *Sound of*

Music, with Julie Andrews had been originally filmed. (The palace was just a short walk from our hotel.)

While on this extraordinary trip, we met a lot of interesting people – some lovely and others ... not so! Beryl and I were dressed in our basic black outfits with pearls, and standing at the entrance to the concert hall, awaiting the opening of the doors. In walked a group of eight British people. We over heard the group's pretentious *grande dame* (a highly respected elderly or middle-aged woman) was informing her entourage, "They're Americans, but they're okay." Whether or not that title was official, she certainly was impressed with herself. It also appeared that the rest of her group was fine with her in that role. As I think back, she was the spitting image of British actress Maggie Smith's portrayal of the dowager (a widow who holds a title to property derived from her deceased husband) in the British Masterpiece Theater Series and later movie: *Downton Abbey,* created by Julian Fellowes.

Those productions took place in the early Twentieth Century. They chronicled the lives of the British aristocratic Crawley family, and their servants, through the era of World War I. The master of the home and family was the only son, who was *Lord of his family's manor*. Think of the Newport Mansions as an example of their type of home. His mother was the Countess Grantham, played brilliantly by British actress Maggie Smith.

Beryl and I were stunned by the dowager's comment ... truly taken aback. We picked our mouths up off the floor, smiled at this group, greeted them politely, and tried being friendly. We indicated that we had just come from enjoying the London sites. Immediately, the dowager asked how we had traveled from London to Salzburg. I told her that "We'd traveled from London to Vienna aboard the Orient Express, and Euro-rail back to Salzburg."

This woman, while looking down her nose at us with disdain, immediately said, "And how might you have been able to afford a trip like that?"

My mouth dropped to the floor once again. The audacity of someone actually asking a question like that. My initial internal reaction was, "None of your dam business!"

Excitedly, Beryl told her: "My friend won the trip on the Orient Express!"

The next exclamation from this self-righteous, haughty woman was, "I have never known anyone who had won anything. How *did you* do that?"

I told her politely about the Eugene O'Neill Theatre and its raffle that I had won. This grande dame was suddenly properly impressed. So much so, she turned to her group, who in turn started making comments such as, "Let me touch your shoulder for good luck."

They all chimed in together and said, "Do tell us all about the Orient Express. Was it as awesome as we've heard?"

We told them about that special train, the early Twentieth Century attire, and then I added: "It turns out that the Orient

Express was continuing its inaugural trip to Budapest and that Prince and Princess Michael of Kent were on board to completion of the journey for the train's celebration."

This tidbit of news was obviously just too much for her. She exclaimed, while once again looking down her nose at we mere Americans *who know nothing about royalty*: "It couldn't possibly have been Prince and Princess Michael!"

At that point their whole group, sounding like magpies, went into discussing why it could not possibly have been those distinguished people. Beryl and I were just standing there looking at each other and occasionally would catch brief phrases as to what they were thinking about this distinguished royal couple. While they were nattering away among themselves for a good five minutes, we would catch phrases referring to the reasons. The proverbial light finally dawned on them. They came condescendingly to the conclusion that, "Just maybe -- it was."

I interjected anxiously: "It was *indeed* Prince and Princess Michael! We had personally met them. Their cabin was at one end of the carriage and ours was at the other. Consequently, at train stops, we would all wander out into the corridor and chat with our neighbors, or if the station stop was long enough, we could get off and continue our chats on the platform. They were really very gracious, down-to-earth and lovely people." (Our snooty socialites were suitably impressed.)

Prince Michael of Kent is a member of the British royal family, younger brother of Prince Edward, Duke of Kent. He is a paternal first cousin of Queen Elizabeth II, and a grandson of King George V and Queen Mary.

Princess Michael of Kent was born Baroness Marie Christine von Reibnitz. She is a member of the British royal family of German, Austrian, and Hungarian nobler descent. Prior to her marriage to Prince Michael, she was an interior designer before becoming an author. She has written several books on European royalty and does lecture tours, as well as supporting her husband in his public duties. We're sure the entourage included these other duties in their dissertation as to why they couldn't possibly have been on the Orient Express with us.

After all that, the doors to the concert hall of Mirabelle Palace were about to open. There were no assigned seats. Since we were first in line, this entourage of folks decided that we *should* go first; they followed on our heels. Apparently, our esteem went up considerably in their judgement. Can you imagine their reaction if we had told them, we had had an audience with the Queen herself? The dowager probably would have fainted on the spot.

***

The only other time I experienced such downright, blatant rudeness was in a visit within our own country. A single friend of mine, Alice, invited me to join her and her parents in their home in Texas. It was a new opportunity for me to visit a state that I had heard a lot about, but had never been to. I flew to Dallas and was met by her and her parents. We drove directly to their lovely home where we had a delicious southern dinner. Following that delectable meal of fried chicken, we were sitting in their living room visiting. Alice's grandmother lived with them, and had joined us for the dinner, as well as the conversation. We were having a delightful discourse about a wide variety of topics: family, weather, sports, careers. All of a sudden, Alice's elderly grandmother looked at me, and stated in her Texas drawl, "You know you're not bad, considering you're a Catholic and a Yankee."

I was stunned. I remember smiling sweetly, but thinking, I'm sure she meant that as a compliment; but, now knowing that I already had two strikes against me before even showing up. It startled me to think, here I was in the south, and from past history I'd thought the Mason-Dixon Line had been buried. Apparently, it hadn't. As we've seen in recent times, immigrants, from Mexico are not always accepted by others. In this case, the majority of Mexicans living in Texas were Catholic. In order for me to attend Mass while there, I was informed, "Why, you'll have to cross the tracks to get to the Catholic Church." The idea didn't bother me. I've always tried to accept and love all people, no matter their nationality, their race, or their creed.

I guess I've always tried to put aside judgmental thoughts about that person who always seems to look down her nose on us. I try to understand the viewpoint of people from different cultural, social or economic backgrounds so that I might see them in a new way. (It doesn't always work.)

***

Please understand that our trip on the fabulous Orient Express was not filled with snooty people. Those who traveled with us were classy, dignified, respectful, and fun human beings.

While aboard the Orient Express, we also met a lovely couple, Geoffrey and Maureen. As it turned out, they were also from Kent, England. Beryl and I kept in touch with them following that memorable trip. I recall a couple of times in particular when they came to New England. Once they were just passing through historic Mystic, Connecticut. I met them there for a lovely dinner. Katie actually had met them when we had traveled to London for the Charles Dickens adventure. Geoffrey and Maureen had driven up to London from Kent to have lunch with us upon our arrival and to spend the afternoon. It was such fun; and they were an absolutely delightful couple — so down to earth.

In late summer of 2000, Geoffrey and Maureen flew into Boston as they were traveling to Maine and eventually Nova Scotia, Canada. That time Beryl and Charlie hosted them for dinner and had included my sister Katie and me, as well. When we arrived at the restaurant, Maureen reminded us all of *Hyacinth Bucket – pronounced 'Bouquet'* -- played perfectly by Patricia Routledge in the British Comedy Series – *Keeping Up Appearances.* In that role, Hyacinth was an artsy snob – putting on airs, while taking control and telling everyone graciously, including her husband, precisely what she thought. In this case, Maureen was also very gracious in directing each of us to where we would sit. We all watched that British comedy and loved

Hyacinth; consequently, we all chuckled to ourselves as Maureen commandeered our seating arrangements.

EPILOGUE

In closing, I share with you my reason for writing this book and its title: *Sunrise – Sunset,* which is based on the music and lyrics from *Fiddler on the Roof,* by Sheldon Harnick and music by Jerry Bock. Music has always been a big part of my life, starting in my younger years with the piano, then onto the violin, voice, and finally the classical guitar.

The lyrics are most appropriate for this autobiography:

"I don't remember growing older...;"
And the Refrain:
"SUNRISE, SUNSET, SUNRISE, SUNSET,
Swiftly flow the days;
Seedlings turn overnight to sunflow'rs,
Blossoming even as we gaze.
SUNRISE, SUNSET, SUNRISE, SUNSET,
Swiftly fly the years;
One season following another,
Laden with happiness and tears."

Those lyrics sum up my life so far and, no doubt, will cover the balance of it as well.

I just love musicals and have been blessed to experience live performances; not only musicals, operas, and a wide variety of shows at our own glorious Garde Arts Center in New London, Connecticut, but also numerous Broadway Shows in New York and in Boston.

To me the most memorable one was *Les Miserable,* based very closely on Victor Hugo's classic novel in 1862. It tells the story of convict Jean Valjean imprisoned for nineteen years all because he stole a loaf of bread in order to feed his sister and her family. When he was finally released from prison, he was not given even a room ... because he was an ex-con.

My sister Katie and I had taken a Show Bus Tour from New London into the City. We were graced with fabulous center front-row seats for that monumental and powerful production – not only did we enjoy the show; but looking into the orchestra pit and observing the musicians was fascinating.

We each had reread the book before going. The book was fabulous and the show was sensational. Being seated in the front row, we felt as if we were right there, back in time, with the performers. I enjoyed the production so much, that following it, I wasn't ready to come back to reality. I was simply in a daze. Yes, we followed the crowd back to our bus, climbed aboard, and found our seats ... but I just sat there ... deaf, dumb, and happy ... not at all ready to return to reality. For years after seeing that awesome production, I didn't want to see the movie or any other rendition of it. It was that special to me!

As previously mentioned, Mom would often wake us around six on a Saturday morning while playing the piano and singing. Of course, she was into the *old songs* from the 1920s -- 40s. She and Pop thoroughly enjoyed listening to Nelson Eddy and Jeannette MacDonald, especially as they sang, *Ah Sweet Mystery of Life.* A couple others of Mom's favorite songs from that period were *Tiptoe Through the Tulips* (pre-Tiny Tim) and *Alice Blue Gown.*

I remember my freshman prom gown was light blue. I felt very special in it while thinking it was "*my* Alice Blue Gown."

I've always loved sunrises and sunsets, as well as rainbows … a double rainbow sends chills down my spine! Whenever I see one, I always think of God being out there with His paint brushes – the richness of the colors and, of course, His artistry. I recall from childhood, across the road from our home, was open pastureland; part of the Ashcraft Farm's forty-three acres. They had a beautiful black horse named Dick. What a glorious memory I have of Dick gracefully galloping across that open space – so peaceful and serene; made even more special with the setting sun.

Unfortunately, over these many years the pasture became woodland. Consequently, we no longer see those gorgeous sunsets from the front of our home. With proper timing, if we drive to the top of the steep hill by us, we can catch those sunsets from there. They are glorious!

Thinking of the beauty of sunrises and sunsets, I'm reminded of one of my daily prayers from *Daily Word,* December 29, 2006, titled: *Thank You, God, for this Day!*

"Thank You, God for this glorious day – a day filled with opportunities to serve You;

To enjoy life; and to express more fully my love for You, myself, and others.

Thank You for the people in my life who support, love and encourage me. I rejoice in every expression they give from their inner divine nature.

I thank You, dear God, for the sacred beauty of nature, for divine creativity expressed in art and music, and for the inspiration of others that speaks to my heart.

Thank You, God, for the strength and wisdom to overcome any challenge in life. In these opportunities to grow, I look to You for guidance. I am uplifted as I connect with

Your loving presence.

Thank you for creating me to be an expression of

Your love in the world."

This special prayer is based on 2 Corinthians 9:15: "Thanks be to God for his indescribable gift!"

My official retirement began October 1, 2017. Since that time, not only have I been concentrating on writing this memoir, but I have been singing in the church choir at Our Lady of Perpetual Help in Quaker Hill, and attempting sporadically to get back to playing my classical guitar. Most importantly, I was spending time with dear friends and family. We were also enjoying a wide variety of concerts at the Garde Arts Center and elsewhere, as well as scrumptious dinners at The Thames Club, often along with fabulous entertainment. I use the past-tense because all of that changed on March 16, 2020, when the Coronavirus Pandemic, which is alleged to have originated in China, hit not only numerous countries around the world ... but our own United States as well.

The world has not seen a pandemic like this since the Spanish Flu in 1918, over one hundred years ago. The similarities from then to now are totally unnerving. For example, while its death toll is unknown, it is generally considered to have been over fifty million. During World War I in Europe, the Flu impacted troops and civilians, and it didn't take long for it to flare up in the United States, where 675,000 people died. Today, we are well on our way to surpassing that number. We have yet to experience the next onset of the Coronavirus, also known as "Covid-19."

In 1918, we had no ICUs. We had no antivirals, no vaccines for Flu. *We had no idea that the Flu was even a virus at that time.* Today we have ICUs, vaccines for Flu … and finally we now have one for this Covid-19. In 1918, they quarantined people in their homes, but likely didn't know if social distancing worked. How could they? Today we know it does. Yes, it is an inconvenience, but it is the most pragmatic thing for individuals to do. It's a way for every person to contribute in helping to fight this virus, for themselves and for others. We need to love *not only ourselves but our neighbors too* -- no matter the color of their skin, ethnic background, nor creed. (Yes, I'm certain we've all read that somewhere: "Love thy neighbor…?")

We are *all* in this together.

From my perspective, I have a hard time comprehending why there is so much resistance to wearing a mask. I believe it is for our own protection and that of others. I do not see it as impinging on my rights. I see it as respecting every human being's right to live, until the good Lord calls each of us home on His terms.

The impact of this pandemic on every citizen has been enormous. People have lost jobs; businesses have closed down or employees are working from home; schools closed with parents becoming teachers overnight for their children; and the stock market has been a yo-yo with its ups and downs. Our government has come up with a little financial relief for people. At least it is something and better than nothing.

While businesses have been closed, or with people working from home, along with the schools being closed, the virus has put a heavy burden on parents. With all of this closeness in often tight quarters, there has been a horrendous increase in the need for the services of Safe Futures, Inc., including dealing with bullying, strangulation, and physical abuse. That agency has been working night and day providing services to women, children, and men. With the required social distancing and overcrowding of their shelters, they have had to resort to putting people up in hotels. That all requires financial resources and lots of teamwork. God bless them for all that they do.

We are so looking forward when Safe Futures, Inc. has its new home in a Family Justice Center, which will bring together all of the necessary coordination of resources (multiple issues including: legal problems, counseling, housing, employment, and education) under one roof – making it easier for the domestic violence victims to get immediate assistance without having to tell their stories over and over again.

I think back to the 1960s, when there was marching and demonstrating for peace. And, yes, some people were holding riots for peace and love, as they are doing all over our country today. The truth of the matter is: there will be no peace until there is true *justice for all people.*

When will we learn that the climate change is impacting us all? As I'm writing this memoir, we've just broken heat records here in Connecticut of thirty-nine days this past summer with temperatures in excess of ninety degrees. (And that was just mid-summer.) In addition, we still had the coronavirus pandemic that all but closed down the country. To my way of thinking, this should *never* happen again. We need to learn from our mistakes and be better stewards of this planet.

I admire the work of Dr. Jane Goodall, English primatologist and anthropologist, who has devoted her life to studying the impact of the humans' disrespect on the environment and on animals. That, too, is impacting our world today, as you will see ...

Dr. Goodall was born in 1934, now age 86, was born Valerie Jane Morris-Goodall. She is considered the world's foremost expert on chimpanzees. She is best known for her sixty-year study of social and family interactions of wild chimpanzees. In 1960, she went to Gombe Stream National Park in Tanzania. Her biography is fascinating; another mentor for women world-wide. She has also founded the Jane Goodall Institute, as well as the Roots & Shoots program.

402

Dr. Goodall has provided us with a grave warning that we need to change our current food systems and to learn from this outbreak. I share a quote from her: "Our disrespect for wild animals can spill over to infect human beings." *She has linked factory farming to the recent rise in antibiotic resistant superbugs.* One further quote from highly regarded Dr. Goodall is: "Humanity is finished if it fails to adapt *after* Covid-19." I couldn't agree more! At 86 years old, Dr. Goodall continues with her noble work.

We are phasing into reopening work places and schools; gradually getting back to normalcy, whenever and whatever that may be. A few pharmaceuticals at warp speed have arrived; we now have a Covid-19 Vaccine to properly protect people here in the U.S.A. and around the world. We are confident this vaccine will help us to resume our lives as we knew them in pre-coronavirus. We pray the vaccine is the magic formula to stop the overwhelming number of deaths in our country and worldwide. In the meantime, most state governments are listening to the scientific experts and distributing the vaccines to everyone.

***

The following addresses what we endured while the world was still in the grip of the Coronavirus Pandemic.

I've always been a woman on the move and a socially motivated individual. I used to find being at home for a long weekend -- without face-to-face contact with friends and the community -- to be almost more than I could handle. During this pandemic, I've adjusted and love being in my own home. I miss being able to greet a dear friend with a hug, and the freedom to go out without having to be sure I have a mask and gloves. Instead, I now do grocery shopping at six o'clock in the morning; the time set aside for senior citizens. And I long for the day when I can once again return to Mass and receive holy communion without having to wear a mask and to socially distance.

***

I'm graced to have traveled as much as I have, which I've addressed in this book. I'm now perfectly content to travel simply

404

within New England (a salute to our breathtaking, magnificent lakes, ocean and views, no matter the season, within our original colonial colonies) especially to Maine and New Hampshire. I specify these two states in particular, as my dear friend and sister, Beryl and I often visit with her family and friends – *my extended family and friends*. I'm now grateful that I no longer have to face busy airports, big crowds, or long lines.

Speaking of Beryl and her family, I'm sorry to say that her husband, dear Charlie, experienced a long illness and was called home in May, 2012. They were living in Florida at the time, having retired there to help with daycare for their grandchildren. Their son and his family had moved from Maine to Florida and were living and working there.

I'll always remember Charlie fondly, who had the most profound, dry Maine sense of humor. He never thought he was funny … but he was. He used to tease me mercilessly about my hats, calling my dapper light blue straw hat, a *horse's hat*. Charlie,

Beryl, their family and mine shared some great times together in Maine, Connecticut, and Florida.

One late afternoon in August, 2015, Beryl and I were chatting on the phone, which we often did. We usually would talk for about an hour; but this time was different. We gabbed for two and a half hours. It was during that conversation a decision was made for the two of us to share my home. It was obvious to us that a greater power had intervened since neither of us had ever thought of our residing together, nor had we even discussed such a possibility. However, as the thought germinated in our minds, we focused on the notion of our endearing longtime friendship, and the power of *camaraderie,* along with our deep faith, to see us through it all. We've always been there for each other, through the good times and the rough patches in our lives too.

Over the next nine months, Beryl sold her home and its contents, while I was preparing my home to welcome her. The gigantic moving van pulled up in front of our home, blocking the view of the house from the road. Consequently, a lot of long-time neighbors mistakenly thought *I* was moving. They didn't know that we had made arrangements to have the movers bring Beryl's car, as well as all of her belongings.

Since we were both alone, it made a lot of sense to us. Of course, we realize that we may not be able to stay living together for the balance of our lives due to health reasons. But we remain optimistic and flexible. In the meantime, we're having a great time together – a true blessing for as long as possible.

***

One thing you probably don't know about me: *I don't like crowds.* Friends have said: "Millie is not the shy and retiring type." I really prefer to get things done and avoid the lime-light as much as possible. I've been truly blessed with recognition in numerous ways for which I am extremely honored and grateful – even being referred to as a "pioneer" or "trailblazer."

Three of the most outstanding recognitions given me:

The *Athena Award* presented by the Greater Mystic, Connecticut Chamber of Commerce in conjunction with Brustolon Buick dealership, which was the first Chamber in Connecticut to make such an award. Eight women were nominated by various organizations and individuals. It was announced at a glorious dinner in May, 2003, that I had been the one selected.

I had been nominated by the SECT Women's Network for not only founding that organization; but having been instrumental in reaching out, teaching, and training other women. Wow! I couldn't believe it. I was totally speechless! One of the benefits, in addition to a beautiful and unique trophy, was the trip to the next Athena Conference in Chicago, Illinois, where I met so many fabulously accomplished women.

We still have a long way to go to achieve total equality in the work place. In the November, 2019 issue of *National Geographic magazine*, one question they posed to Ellen Pao, was "What is the most important challenge that women face today?" (Ms. Pao is running *Project Include,* a nonprofit she founded to foster inclusion and diversity in the tech world.) She is quoted as saying, "Being treated equitably, based on ability to contribute, based on skills. Being accepted as equal. "

The second time when my socks were knocked off, and I was rendered speechless, was in November, 2014 when Lawrence + Memorial Hospital totally surprised me at their annual Well-Healed Woman event, by recognizing me as the Sixth Annual *Well-Healed Woman*. Wow! While the prior recipients of this distinguished award had been directly affiliated with the healthcare world, I was recognized for my *volunteer work*, having served on their Board of Directors, as well as numerous committees.

After retiring and while beginning to work on this autobiography, I received the third knock your socks off recognition. The Waterford Education Foundation honored me on May 18, 2018 at a fund-raising dinner by establishing the Millie Devine Scholarship to a Waterford High School graduating senior who has been very much involved in the community. The first of these scholarships was presented at the Waterford High School

Seniors Awards Night in June, 2018 to an extremely talented and deserving young lady, Sophie Wang. What an honor for me to be there that night, as they announced her individual academic and community accomplishments, as well as her plans for continuing her education at Dartmouth. I am confident she has a successful life ahead.

Obviously, each year as this scholarship is awarded, I continue experiencing that special honor, feeling proud of the accomplishments of my alma mater, its graduates, and recognition of my own small impact. It certainly brings back precious memories from my years at Waterford High 1956 - 1960.

As we all know, no one can do everything without help from a wide variety of resources. The talent may be shared by co-workers, family, or friends. I am grateful to everyone who has been of assistance to me over these many, many years. I offer a great BIG thank you to all of you!

In the November, 2019 issue of *National Geographic,* Oprah Winfrey was asked: "What is the greatest hurdle you've overcome? Her response: "The *disease* to please. It happens when we are not raised to know our own value and our own worth." Unfortunately, her statement is so true. Each of us must take responsibility for our own lives and be the best we can possibly be. We must keep growing throughout our entire lives – never giving up, and never succumbing to fear.

I've had a lot of fun working with so many different people; whether it was serving on a wide variety of non-profit boards, building community foundations, restoring the Garde Arts Center, or hosting Devine Planning's First Anniversary High Tea in the lobby of Harris Place catered by then Carolyn Johnson's fabulous Tea Room & Gift Shop.

I've been blessed in traveling to national secretaries' conventions, banking conventions, Soroptimist and Rotary International conventions, which have taken me near and far. I've been graced by meeting people from all walks of life and cultures.

It is a privilege to work with these fabulous individuals on grass-roots goals, such as stamping out polio worldwide.

I even dabbled in politics by being appointed to the Waterford Charter Commission, as well as being a member of and serving on the Board of the New London Development Corporation.

When I think back to my youth, while growing up in this area, downtown New London was the major shopping area for us, and where we had to go for doctors, dentists, lawyers, banks, accountants, groceries -- plus any other business matters requiring attention. Our only other choice was to go to downtown Norwich for such services, or all the way to our capital city of Hartford.

I've never been afraid to dream what may have appeared to be *The Impossible Dream.* Of course, that wonderful song came from the famous Broadway show: *Man of La Mancha.*

Whenever I've been told "You cannot do that," my attitude has always been, *"We'll just see about that."* I can be very determined – some may even say stubborn – but I've always considered myself a visionary and a doer.

Speaking of *doers,* I am saddened deeply by the death of the distinguished Justice Ruth Bader Ginsburg, on September 18, 2020, at age 87. She was such a champion of women's rights: a trailblazer as a civil-rights attorney, who chipped away at discriminatory practices, and as the second woman to serve on the Supreme Court, she has become an icon for us all.

As Gloria Steinem, age 86, another fabulous trailblazer, icon, proponent of women's rights said about Justice Ruth Bader Ginsburg: "She was my teacher in so many ways. Day by day, I want to say to myself, 'What would Ruth do?' If I do that, if I ask myself that question, and do my best to do it, then Ruth will still be here. And I hope a lot of us can do that, everyone who knew or saw or honored her."

I believe whole heartedly in helping others. In my retirement I have been concentrating my time and energy working with two

413

very special non-profits: Lawrence + Memorial Hospital, arm of Yale-New Haven Healthcare -- and Safe Futures, Inc., and, of course, the church I regularly attend, Our Lady of Perpetual Help.

When I was forced to take early retirement from Fleet Bank -- devastating to me at age fifty-five as I have already described -- I hadn't planned on retiring. I had no "after retirement plans" for any such thing. I knew I needed to do something, because I firmly believed I had much to offer. However, I did *not* want to go to another big bank. Community banks didn't have trust departments at that time.

I had found my niche in the trust business and being of service to others. I loved the diversity of what I was doing. I learned so much and was thrilled with my successful career. Of course, there were rocky times; but the good certainly outweighed the bad. As Reba McIntire said in her book, *REBA: My Story:* "One of the best things about success – sharing it and bringing happiness to those you love." She also said she never gave up on herself: "And that's a piece of hard-won wisdom I'd pass on to anyone wanting to chase a dream."

I'll always treasure that quip of wisdom from Reba.

I've never been one to dwell on unpleasant experiences, and have always had a strong faith in God. I have experienced over the years sexual harassment and prejudice for being: *a woman, a Yankee, and a Catholic.* Yes, those insidious looks or winks as you walk into a male's office that would have been more appropriate at a cocktail party. Or thinking back to the quote I shared from Alice's grandmother: "You know, you're not bad since you're a Yankee and a Catholic." I've dealt head-on with those encounters. I feel such empathy for the people who have not been able to cope with such mistreatment.

At the time I knew I was actually retiring from Fleet Bank, I made a promise to myself that: *I was only going to do – what is fun, what I love doing, and being of service to others.*

415

As Mother Teresa once said: "We must know that we have been created for greater things, not just to be a number in the world. We have been created in order to love and to be loved."

Keep in mind that truly humble people are centers of peace ... because they fear neither their own failure nor others' success.

As the song says, and I'm paraphrasing: "Sunrise – Sunset swiftly fly the years ... laden with happiness and tears." As I've said, I've been truly blessed; I look forward with great anticipation to what lies ahead.

God bless every one of you who has now read this memoir and, hence, has joined me in benefiting Safe Futures, Inc.

I close with the words to a very old endearing hymn: *Have I Done Any Good?* It follows the theme of Mom's, her sisters', and my adopted lifetime motto: *Let me live in a house by the side of the road and be a friend to mankind."*

Have I Done Any Good?
Have I done any good in the world today?
Have I helped anyone in need?

Have I cheered up the sad and made someone feel glad?
If not, I have failed indeed.
Has anyone's burden been lighter today
Because I was willing to share?
Have the sick and the weary been helped on their way?
When they needed my help was I there?

Refrain:
Then wake up and do something more
Than dream of your mansion above.
Doing good is a pleasure, a joy beyond measure,
A blessing of duty and love.

There are chances for work all around just now,
Opportunities right in our way.
Do not let them pass by … Saying, "Sometime I'll try,"
But go and do something today.
'Tis noble of man to work and to give;
Love's labor has merit along.
Only he who does something helps others to live.
To God each good work will be known.

Refrain:
Then wake up and do something more
Than dream of your mansion above.
Doing good is a pleasure, a joy beyond measure,
A blessing of duty and love.

FINIS.

Author's Note: While we have reached the end of my autobiography and can say: **FINIS**, that only applies to this book, NOT my life. I still have a lot of living to do....

ACKNOWLEDGEMENTS

I am eternally grateful to several people who have worked very closely with me in completing this autobiography. First, I thank Jeanne Sigel, who has been a long-time friend, and involved extensively in the Southeastern Connecticut communities. She has also owned her own business, Island Design, a highly regarded marketing firm. She designed the logo and stationery for my business: Devine Planning. Jeanne not only encouraged me but insisted that I *had* to write this book. She was not going to take "NO" for an answer ... she even offered to help me -- and she has.

Jeanne's husband, Steve Sigel, has been the Executive Director of the Garde Arts Center. since 1988. He very successfully resurrected it from the rubble and ruins it had nearly become. Now it stands proudly at the top of State Street; the pride of New London. Jeanne and Steve Sigel are individually fabulous people and quite a unique team.

Jeanne and Steve did me a huge favor by introducing me to Nicholas Checker, who has become my writing coach. He is an absolute gem, a treasure trove of knowledge, and extremely talented. Nick is a graduate of the University of Connecticut, an author, a playwright, and a filmmaker. His latest book is, *The Saga of Marathon*. Yes, he is Greek, a marathon runner, and a former gymnastics coach.

Nick has learned all about writing from studying the classics: novels, movies, productions, and so forth. I cannot begin to thank him enough for guiding someone like me -- who had only done business writing for over fifty years -- in creating this autobiography.

I started this book when I first retired from Dime Bank in October, 2017 by laying out what I wanted to cover -- in chronological order. Not only has Nick seen me through this whole learning process; but my dear friend and sister, Beryl Hobart has too. She knows the angst and the joy I endured in creating this memoir. I am so grateful to her for bearing with me and not interrupting while I attempted to get my thoughts on paper. She has also been a sounding-board for me, as I read section-after-section-after-section to her. Beryl also shared with me her own experiences, especially regarding the Boston Strangler; for, she and I had shared that extremely stressful time in Boston.

I also thank Alan Thibodeau for helping Jeanne Sigel and me with the formatting of this book and guidance in our interaction with Amazon in its publishing. Self-publishing is quite an involved process and a whole new learning experience. Thank you, Alan!

I thank Gil Shasha, retired prominent litigating attorney. He retired after forty years of fighting his clients' cases before juries. While I knew of him then, I've become enamored with his charm and meaningful public readings of excerpts from my autobiography. You see, Nick Checker's style, when we don't have a pandemic going on, is to engage professional readers for his budding authors' works. We usually would have a "finale" reading every two-three-months. At this point, our last one was in January, 2020; the pandemic hit us in March, just before our last scheduled one. These readings are most helpful to rising new authors, because they provide immediate feedback from the intimate audiences of Nick's students, whether private or group classes. These writers get to hear their own works read out loud. The audience feedback is invaluable.

I have been blessed by Gil's having read most of my works, and reactions from attentive audiences have been shared so willingly and graciously, for which I am most grateful. Gil is a professional and reads with such a depth of understanding, compassion, knowledge, and expression. Believe me, if I'd ever needed a litigating attorney and was facing a jury, I'd want him on my side.

I thank my family and friends, especially those included in my autobiography, for all of their support: Beryl Hobart, Henry Savin, Tom and Valerie Ostronic, Tristan and Rebecca Scholl Ostronic, Lori Reynolds, Kathleen Verano, and Melissa Zaitchik. Both Kathleen and Melissa are professionals with Safe Futures, Inc.

And I thank *you*, the most important readers, for your interest in my memoir and for helping our fellow men, women and children, who have had the misfortune to need to deal with so many of the horrors in life of bullying, strangulation, and physical abuse. No one should ever have to deal with such atrocities. Thank God for the good works of Safe Futures and other social service agencies of assistance in numerous ways.

I also echo American country singer, songwriter, and actress Reba McIntire's sentiments: "Thank you, God, for letting me keep my sanity and my memory long enough to finish this book. I'm glad it all started with You."

Author's Note: Please note that the proceeds from the sale of this book are ALL going to Safe Futures, Inc., 16 Jay Street, New London, CT 06320 for the continuance and fulfillment of their crucial mission, which is as follows:

(From the Safe Futures Web Site: www.safefuturesct.org)

- 24-hour Law Enforcement Lethality Assessment (LAP) Line
- Genesis House Emergency Shelter
- Criminal Court Advocates New London and Norwich
- Victim Advocate Law Enforcement (VALE) Norwich Police Department

Restoring Hope:

- Walk in Counseling Offices—New London and Norwich, CT
- Civil Court Advocate New London and Norwich
- Support Groups
- Restorative Practices
- Essentials Donation Center for Necessities, Emergency Clothing & Household Goods

Changing the Future:

- Phoenix House Transitional Housing
- Scattered Site Transitional Housing
- Violence is Preventable Educators in school class rooms
- Engaging Men
- Career Center

The following history is taken from the web site of Safe Futures, Inc.: http://safefuturesct.org:

- "Founded in 1976 as the Women's Center of Southeastern Connecticut, Safe Futures began as an information and referral service for women entering the workforce. When a rape crisis hotline was added to the services offered, it soon became clear that the perpetrators of the assaults were men the callers knew – their husbands and boyfriends. This realization led to the opening of several safe houses, and eventually a permanent emergency shelter in 1978.

- As demand for the Women's Center's services grew, so did its programs and expertise in the field of domestic violence. In 2012, the Women's Center changed its name to Safe Futures to better reflect those being served by the agency as well as its full scope of programs. The agency serves all 21 cities and towns in southeastern Connecticut.

Since learning of this prayer in 1995, it is included in my own daily prayers:

Prayer for Life

Pope John Paul II

Evangelium Vitae, 1995

O Mary, bright dawn of the new world, Mother of the living, to you do we entrust the cause of life: Look down, O Mother, upon the vast numbers of babies not allowed to be born, of the poor whose lives are made difficult, of men and women who are victims of brutal violence, of the elderly and the sick killed by indifference or out of misguided mercy. Grant that all who believe in your Son may proclaim the Gospel of life with honesty and love to the people of our time. Obtain for them the grace to accept that Gospel as a gift ever new, the joy of celebrating it with gratitude throughout their lives and the courage to bear witness to it resolutely, in order to build, together with all people of good will, the civilization of truth and love, to the praise and glory of God, the Creator and lover of life. Amen

A WORD ABOUT THE AUTHOR: MILDRED E. DEVINE

Millie received a Bachelor of Arts with honors in Business Administration from Upper Iowa University, Fayette, Iowa. She is a graduate of the National Graduate Trust School at Northwestern University in Evanston, Illinois. She was a Certified Trust and Financial Advisor (CTFA) and an Accredited Estate Planner® (AEP®).

She worked for the Trust & Investment Group of Shawmut Bank (now Bank of America) in various capacities for 32 years, retiring as Vice President in January, 1997. During her career she administered four private foundations for about twenty years. Millie had her own business, Devine Planning 1997-2012; During that time, she also worked as a trust officer for Dime Bank, 2007-17.

Millie has always been involved in civic and professional organizations, having served as President of the Estate and Tax Planning Council of Eastern Connecticut and numerous other professional and social services boards. She is a Paul Harris Fellow with sapphire awards, and a past president of the New London Rotary Club. She is also the founder, past president, and still a member of the Southeastern Connecticut Women's Network. Millie currently volunteers with Safe Futures, Inc., at the Lawrence + Memorial Hospital, and at her church, Our Lady of Perpetual Help.

Made in the USA
Middletown, DE
11 July 2021